**Jobs and Careers after A levels and equivalent advanced qualifications** – ninth edition

Published by Lifetime Publishing, Mill House, Stallard Street, Trowbridge BA14 8HH

© Nord Anglia Lifetime Development South West Ltd, 2007

ISBN 978-1904979210

Printed and bound by Cromwell Press Ltd, Trowbridge

Cover design by Jane Norman

Illustrations by Royston Robertson

# Contents

# About the author

Beryl Dixon is an experienced careers adviser who has worked for different careers companies and in a tertiary college, where she helped students aged 16-19 with their decisions on both higher education and employment. She has also worked for the Ministry of Defence and the Department for Children, Schools and Families (DCSF), visiting schools in Brussels, Luxembourg, Cyprus and Hong Kong to provide careers advice to the children of expatriate service personnel and government officials. She now concentrates on careers writing and is the author of several books.

# Acknowledgements

Many thanks to all the people who were happy for their stories to be told as case studies for this book, and thanks also to the organisations and companies that helped to identify suitable staff to feature.

# Introduction

This book is written for students taking, or who have already gained, **level 3 qualifications** (as defined in the National Qualifications Framework for England, Wales and Northern Ireland) or the equivalent qualification level in Scotland.

## What are level 3 qualifications?

Any of the following:

- A levels
- Scottish Highers/Advanced Highers*
- BTEC National qualifications
- AVCE/Advanced GNVQ/GSVQ level III (all now replaced by newer qualifications but still valid)
- NVQ or SVQ level 3.

For a long time A levels or Highers in traditional subjects were seen, in the main, as stepping stones to higher education. Entry to degree, Higher National Diploma (HND) and other full-time courses depended on these examination results, and most 18- or 19-year-olds used them as a ticket to university and college. Then came an increase in the number of other full-time programmes of study that could also lead to higher education – National Diplomas and Certificates in many subjects (which still exist), and Advanced General National or General Scottish Vocational Qualifications (which don't). They died a death to be replaced by A levels or Highers in applied subjects. The number of vocational degree and diploma courses in universities and higher education colleges has also mushroomed. As a result, more and more young people are now staying on in education after 16, and then proceeding to higher education. And, as the number of job applicants with higher qualifications grows, more and more employers are looking to graduates and HND holders to fill even their junior management posts.

Yet many 18- and 19-year-olds with level 3 qualifications do look for and find employment every year.

Everyone now studying for level 3 qualifications needs to make a positive decision about the next step. Full-time higher education doesn't have to

*Under the Scottish qualifications framework these are level 6 and 7 qualifications respectively, but are broadly equivalent to level 3 in the National Framework for England, Wales and Northern Ireland. Throughout this book, level 3 qualifications should be interpreted to include these equivalent-level Scottish qualifications.

be an automatic choice. The fact that you are reading this book means that you are at least considering the possibility of not going on to a higher-education course.

- You may have had enough of study and don't want to face the prospect of another two to four years in full-time education.
- Possibly, the hope of an exciting job at 18 is much more appealing to you.
- Perhaps it is the prospect of a regular salary cheque that attracts you?
- It may be that you have already taken your exams and did not perform as well as you had hoped. Rather than accepting a place on a course that doesn't really inspire you, or re-sitting your exams, you would prefer to look for work.
- Or, it may be the expense of higher education that deters you? Grants are available only to students on low incomes; tuition fees have to be paid – and the average student graduates with debts of around £13,000. (See Chapter one for more on this.)

Whatever your reason for not entering higher education, there are alternatives. However, whereas it is easy to find details about degree and other courses, there is far less written information on job opportunities. This book, now in its ninth edition and revised to reflect the current job market, has been designed to help you find out about the opportunities open to you.

It should also give you insights – in particular, through the career profiles in this book – into the routes to employment that other people have taken. The book isn't another job-finding manual. Although you will find some tips on applying for jobs and surviving interviews, you will need to consult other sources for further information and advice. (Some suggestions are given.) Rather, the book aims to open your eyes to job possibilities at 18-19 and to explain what you can expect in the way of training when you first start work.

In looking for employment, you need to give careful consideration to where a particular job could lead you. Training can play a very important part here. After all, you will not want to end up in a 'dead-end' job but in one in which you can make progress (i.e. a career). So, trying to look ahead now could make the difference between getting just a job or just the job for you!

This book could trigger off an idea that you had not previously considered.

# Chapter one

## So you want a job?

## Or do you?

Although you are reading this book you may not yet have reached a decision about your next step. You could simply be skipping through to see what the options might be. Fine – and hopefully you will feel in a better position to make the decision between full-time higher education and employment. Did you notice the use of the word 'full-time'? All the evidence suggests that people with a higher-education qualification behind them do better in the job and salary stakes. But no one says that they must study full time. If you want to progress, you should be giving serious consideration to part-time courses. That's right. Study for a qualification while you are at work. This is a world apart from leaving school or college and going into a dumb job with no prospects!

Studying part time isn't easy. You'll see that when you read some of the case studies. Also – are you sure that you want to miss out on the experience of student life? And work demands a level of maturity. Several people who appear as case studies in this book are responsible for the work of older colleagues. That isn't always easy either. But you would be surprised at how much your confidence would improve as you gained experience and job skills.

## What are the advantages and disadvantages of full-time higher education?

For

- Time to enjoy yourself and spread your wings without the pressure of having to learn a job.
- Chance to leave home for a relatively structured environment – i.e. a transition period.
- Opportunity to make friends from different areas and backgrounds – many of whom you'll keep for life.
- Possibility of keeping your options open. You don't have to decide on a career yet.
- OR – if you do know what career you want and will choose a vocational degree or diploma – you will have more time to do your academic work.
- In other words, more free time.

Against

- Not seeing any relevance to what you study.
- You might still have to do a lengthy training when you leave university.
- Having to leave home, whether you want to do so or not, if the course is not available locally.
- Losing several years' earnings.
- Missing out on work experience.
- Student debt!

## And employment?

### For

- The chance to combine earning with learning. Seeing the relevance of theory to practice every day.

- Making an early start to a career.

- No student debt – but a salary instead.

### Against

- You might make a mistake and choose a job you don't like. (But then, that could happen at any stage.)

- Curtailed social life. You'll have to fit in time for course work related to studying for qualifications.

- You are likely to be restricted to employment opportunities available in your home area. (Graduates are usually more mobile because their starting salaries are higher.)

# Finance

Full-time higher education will cost you money. All but a handful of universities now charge the maximum 'top up' tuition fee of £3070 a year (2007/2008). Fees need not be paid until students have graduated and are in reasonably-paid employment. There are loans – and grants for students from less well-off backgrounds to help with living costs. But the fact remains that students who enter higher education from 2007 onwards can expect a higher level of debt than their predecessors, whose fees were around £1100.

## How much money?

The trouble is that you will get different answers according to whom you ask! Also, individuals' expenditure differs and what one student considers essential expenses will be someone else's luxury items. However, for what it's worth:

- NatWest conducted a survey in June 2006 and discovered that the average student debt on graduation was £13,252

- the National Union of Students (NUS) quoted £13,501 in 2005.

Neither of these figures of course includes the increased tuition fees, which came in after the surveys were conducted.

- The Department for Children, Schools and Families (DCSF) said that the above figures were too high, but had no up-to-date ones of its own. Officials were, however, quoted in *The Sunday Times* in 2005 as saying that they expected average student debt to rise to £15,000 from 2006.

- The NUS' estimate of debt level is 'as much as £33,708 by 2010'.

The average starting salary for graduates in 2006, according to NatWest, was £13,860. Now this contrasts very strongly with other much-touted sums. Again, it depends on whom you ask. Some surveys use figures supplied by the Association of Graduate Recruiters. This sounds like an official organisation. It is – but its members are blue-chip companies, which do pay higher salaries to their recruits. The association therefore does not cover all the employers graduates are working for. So, although some lucky graduates are enjoying starting salaries of over £35,000, they are in the minority.

And the problem with surveys is that many of them concentrate on starting salaries. What is needed is more up-to-date and comprehensive research on the effect of a higher-education qualification over a lifetime's earnings. Those done to date all confirm that over a working life graduates do better than other people. But there is some feeling that the figure by which they do so is decreasing. A 2006 survey from Swansea University found that men with a degree could expect to see their lifetime earnings increased by £141,539 compared with those with A levels; for women the bonus would be £157,982. With more graduates entering the labour market, employers simply don't have to pay the same premium they used to in the past.

So there you are!

According to the Government, 43% of the 18- to 19-year-old age group now choose higher education. The Government's aim is actually that 50% of young people aged 18-30 *should experience* higher education by the year 2010. But that is somewhat vaguely worded! And they haven't defined what 'experience' means. It could mean through part-time courses. And it is possible to go as far as degree level through this route. In addition there are lots of Higher National Diploma courses available that are specifically related to jobs. Don't worry. You will not be pushed into full-time higher education against your will.

If 43% of your age group enrol for full-time higher education courses it looks, doesn't it, as though you should have no problem in walking into a job? 'What competition is there?', you might be thinking. If more people each year are flocking to university and college, that surely leaves more jobs for those who don't?

### But wait a minute!

You are still going to be competing with:

- over half of your own age group

- younger employees who left school at 16 and gained experience either in a job or through work-based training, some of whom, two or three years on, may be under consideration for promotion to supervisory or junior management-level work

- people leaving higher education. Some employers now prefer graduates for training schemes for which they previously recruited applicants with level 3 qualifications. In other cases, careers that were once open to people with level 3 qualifications now have a degree or Higher National Diploma as their minimum entry requirement.

So, you could find yourself squeezed by competition from both older applicants with higher qualifications, and younger people with lower qualifications than your own.

# The job seekers: which is your group?

Job seekers with level 3 qualifications usually fall into one of four groups.

1. Those who know from the outset that they want a job rather than higher education.

2. Those who do not get the exam grades they need, fail to get a place on the higher education course they want and who do not want to re-sit their exams.

3. Those who begin a course in higher education, then drop out.

4. Some older students who are taking exams with a view to re-entering the job market or making a career change.

If you are in group 1 you have a head start. Why?

Because of the following points.

- You have plenty of time to look around and make plans while other students are busily filling in university and college application forms.

- You should be in time to apply to companies offering training schemes that have closing dates (notably retail management and some commercial training programmes) as early as January or February.

- You are applying with a more positive attitude – i.e. it is obvious to employers that you are motivated and not using employment as a last resort.

If you are in this group, do make sure you put to good use the time you have. It's tempting to sit back and let life pass by while your friends are concentrating on UCAS and other higher-education application forms.

Ask for a careers interview well before Christmas, so that you can get some ideas together and do not miss out on any important closing dates.

If you're in group 2 or 3, you may face some initial disadvantages.

- You might be less immediately attractive to employers. (Are you going for second best?)

- Your timing could be wrong. School or college leavers will be dependent on suitable jobs coming up from August onwards, so if you didn't expect to be looking for a job you will be making a late start. On the positive side, however, some employers deliberately recruit in the late summer when they know that there are 18+ leavers around who are not going to university but who, nevertheless, achieved very reasonable exam results. Remember that your choice of options may depend on how much your exam results fell short of your expectations – i.e. just how 'badly' did you actually do?

For those in group 3, leaving university or college mid-year could mean that you become available just when an employer does have a suitable vacancy and there are no school- or college-leavers available to apply. On the other hand, you might be deciding to leave at a time when no one seems to be recruiting. (In that case you can always get a temporary job until something better comes along.)

Older students – group 4 – may have particular difficulties if they are tied to a geographical area (see the section on 'Mobility' later in this chapter).

Some of the people whose career profiles appear in this book made applications simultaneously to employers and to higher-education institutions. In this way, they were able to keep their options open, in some cases making the final decision only after receiving their exam results. Henry Marshall (page 217) and Emma Turner (page 100) come into this category, while Melanie Helps (page 93) and Louise Matson (page 128) both sent in UCAS forms but later changed their minds and withdrew from the UCAS scheme. Justin Randall (page 147) and Lyndsey Taggart (page 159) intended to apply – but to do so during a gap year. Both changed their minds during the year.

A few people make reference to the fact that they were glad to have kept their options open. Others were adamant that they would not fill in a UCAS form even as a safety measure, and resisted all pressure to do so. Fiona Catling (page 144), Alex Hargreaves (page 230) Fiona King (page 91), Matthew Morfoot (page 206), Kieri White (page 165), Jake Wilks (page 209) and Rob Wilson (page 115) did not apply to university at all. They knew that they wanted to follow the work-based training route from the outset. Samantha Hubbard (page 183), Sarah Gallimore (page 171), Gemma Lawson (page 213) and Gemma Wright (page 178) all started degree courses before leaving for different reasons.

Students often complain about the quality of advice and help they received at school or college, where all the attention seemed to be given to the ones heading for university. In some cases, this criticism is justified. Schools and colleges tend to be judged by their success rate in getting pupils into higher education, particularly to university, rather than on the numbers gaining employment. In other cases, students may have been unduly sensitive to the fact that the university and college entrance system forces staff to give priority in the autumn term of year 13 to UCAS applicants. If they haven't got their forms in by the middle of January, they are too late. Consequently, it may be that for a term at least, those students are given priority.

However, there is no excuse for schools not to arrange careers advice for job seekers. To repeat a point made earlier – ask for an appointment with the personal/careers adviser from the local Connexions/careers service who visits your school or college. It is their job to provide advice on all aspects of career choice, including both higher-education routes and immediate employment prospects. What is more, part of their job involves visiting employers, so they know what is available.

If no personal adviser/careers adviser visits your school or college, look up 'careers' or 'Connexions' in the phone book and make an appointment to visit their office.

N.B. Careers information and advice are provided, depending on where you live, by local offices of:

- the Connexions service in England
- the Careers service, Northern Ireland
- Careers Scotland
- Careers Wales.

## Taking stock

Now that you have decided on, or are considering, employment as an option, what are the possibilities and what information should you have?

Is it true that employers require much lower grades than universities and colleges? Of what value are your particular subjects?

Basically, you will require the following information:

- the types of employment open to people with level 3 qualifications
- the kind of training you would receive
- when and how to apply – this is very important.

For information on jobs, see Chapter two, which looks at opportunities in detail. For hard information on what it is really like starting work read through the career profiles that might interest you. Job-hunting is dealt with in Chapter three, and for hints on job applications see Chapter four. Training is discussed in Chapter five.

## Entry requirements

The entry requirement for some jobs, particularly those with formal training schemes that incorporate day release or other forms of training for professional qualifications, is the same as for some higher-education courses – for example a minimum of two A levels/three Highers or a pass in a National Diploma. Particular GCSEs/S grades may also be stipulated – most commonly, English language and maths.

You could find that some employers are not too worried about high grades in examinations, so making a career start with them can be easier than getting a higher-education place. A job advertisement may simply state the level of qualification required without stipulating grades.

But, be warned...

Some employers – usually those recruiting in popular job areas – will ask for high grades. Applicants for training in chartered accountancy, for example, are likely to find that the equivalent of 240 UCAS points is required, as this is the recommendation of the Institute of Chartered Accountants.

You should also be aware that employers look beyond educational qualifications and will be very interested in the personal qualities you can offer – such as communication skills, leadership potential and the ability to work in a team.

# Job prospects

What, realistically, are your chances of getting a job?

Destination figures are not collected for people leaving the education system with level 3 qualifications in the same way as they are for those leaving higher education. Universities collect their own statistics on students graduating in different subjects several months after they have left. Schools and colleges are required to produce immediate destination statistics, but afterwards, 18-year-old leavers may visit Connexions/careers centres or their Jobcentre Plus (all of which do keep statistics) or may look for work through other sources including private-sector recruitment agencies and the internet. There is no single source of information and it is difficult, therefore, to get an overall picture of those looking for work.

There are several factors that affect your chances of getting a job – particularly if your choice is restricted to one or two occupations.

## The economic climate

We all know that some regions suffer higher levels of unemployment than others. There is strong competition in some areas for jobs offering good training.

## Geographical area

The availability of jobs varies greatly in different parts of the country. In some areas, a lot of recruitment may be taking place; in others, very little.

The types of jobs available also depend on the nature of local employment. You will probably know which are the largest industries and businesses near to you. If you live in a manufacturing area, there may be little chance of finding an opening in rural estate surveying; in seaside resorts there may be openings in tourism and catering, but not much opportunity to get into civil engineering or construction management. Small towns don't have large factories with openings for trainees in work study or quality control, advertising agencies or airports – and so on.

Nevertheless, companies employ a lot of different people and may have openings in career fields other than the most immediately obvious. If your nearest large employer is a pharmaceutical company, that company doesn't just employ laboratory staff. It may recruit trainee accountants and administrators and, possibly, trainees for computing, management services, company secretarial, personnel, legal and marketing work. The product it makes is immaterial.

Sometimes job prospects depend on local employers' preferences rather than availability of a particular type of employment. There is, for example, an Apprenticeship route towards a housing management career, but some employers prefer trainees to have relevant degrees or Higher National Diplomas.

Similarly, you could qualify as a town planner by a part-time route, but many councils' planning departments prefer to take trainees with degrees. It is possible to become a trainee journalist with GCSEs/S grades (rare), level 3 qualifications or a degree, but it is up to individual editors to decide whom to recruit.

## Mobility

Salary prospects at 18 don't always make leaving home a viable option, and you may therefore have to choose from a restricted range of local employers.

However, some large employers – those that recruit nationally – may expect applicants to be prepared to work anywhere. The Civil Service is one such employer. Others include the Armed Forces, the police and some national retail chains, which see exposure to buying and selling patterns in different regions of the country as a necessary part of training. If you apply to such employers, you will find entry difficult, if not impossible, if you refuse to move away from your home area. But the employers do either pay high enough salaries to enable you to live independently, or provide or subsidise your accommodation.

# Your choice

Having read your way through some of these points, you may be wondering if you really have much choice! Yes, you do – but within limitations. You should not be steam-rollered into applying for a degree or diploma place you do not want. Higher education will not go away.

It will still be there in a few years' time if you are qualified and want it. Melanie Helps (page 93) talks about doing an Open University degree before she is 30. Louise Matson (page 128) has started to look for part-time degrees in her field of hotel management. Alex Hargreaves (page 230) says that he is not yet ready to return to study, but if and when he is his company will encourage him and help financially with an HND or degree course. Fiona King (page 91) also intends to study for a degree on a part-time basis.

If you decide to do a higher-education course in a few years you will not need to feel out of place. Greater numbers of mature students enrol on higher-education courses every year. But by choosing the employment route now, you will have to:

- bear in mind that certain careers will not be open to you

- expect competition when applying for jobs

- expect to have to give up some of your free time in order to study for qualifications in a job (see Chapter five)

- start acquiring information about possible openings as soon as possible

- accept that you may not get your first choice of job.

The last point, however, is something that applies to everyone, not just school and college leavers. Many successful professionals, including those with degrees, were unsuccessful in applying for their first-choice jobs. The career profiles in this book include several people who are now happily settled in a second-choice career. Sarah Goodridge (page 192) would have liked to join the RAF but was prevented from doing so by her eyesight. Henry Marshall (page 217) worked in retailing before he got his dream job in air traffic control; Phillip Mann (page 202) trained as a graphic designer but had to re-think when he could not find a job. He is now a successful estate agent. Will McAlpine (page 135) initially thought about law but now manages a building society branch and Heidi Schulz (page 155) worked in industry before joining the police force.

Remember: you don't have to stick with your first choice. All is well that ends well. It is no disgrace to leave a job (or course) if you have given it a fair trial and it is not working out. In any case, the days of spending 40 years with one employer in return for a gold watch have gone. Job mobility is a fact of life. Many people will have to consider retraining at some stage in their careers, and the guarantee of a job for life is something very few of us can now count on. If you retrain a little earlier than some people, what does it matter?

Some of the people who feature in this book had already spent some time on a higher-education course before realising that they had made a mistake. Samantha Hubbard (page 183) spent a year at university then entered the career that she had already chosen – but as an 18+ entrant rather than as a graduate. Gemma Wright (page 178) actually spent two years on a degree course before deciding that she had made a mistake. Gemma Lawson (page 213) had completed two years of a degree course before leaving for personal reasons.

## The people who agreed to be featured in this book

They have been chosen to represent a wide range of jobs. They are also at different stages in their careers. Some of them have just left school or college; others are coming towards the end of their training. And others are firmly established in their careers and have been promoted one or more times. They have been included so that you can see some of the career prospects for people who start out with 18+ qualifications.

Obviously, they are happy with their decisions. Otherwise they wouldn't be here. So there are no quotes from people who feel they have made a mistake and should have opted for the full-time higher-education route. But this is what some of them have to say:

*'I decided that I wanted to get some real job experience before committing to a university course. Also, I did not want to get into debt when I was unsure of what I wanted to do at the end of a degree course.'*

*Melanie Helps, Civil Servant*

'I was not a university type of person and wanted a more practical start to my career.'

*Lindsay Currie, library assistant*

'The main difference for me was being taught in a work environment, rather than learning the theory in isolation. Being able to apply on a daily basis what I was learning on the AAT course was far more useful. I'm working. I'm enjoying it and I'm earning money, instead of going to university and ending up in debt three years' later.'

*Fiona Catling, accounting technician*

'I found a job that enabled me to learn and to work out where I could go next. It opened doors for me. I would advise people to spend plenty of time looking into their options and not to feel rushed into making a decision.'

*Sally Parker, compliance analyst*

'Remember that within many organisations there are lots of opportunities to take relevant courses and achieve qualifications. For instance, I have the chance to take the Chartered Institute of Marketing's Certificate because it is relevant to the work that I do.'

*Sarah Gallimore, project assistant*

'I enjoy everything about my work – and learning on the job with what I am learning backed up by academic study one day a week is exactly the right route for me. Plus I am earning a salary and I shall not have any student debts to pay off.'

*Matthew Morfoot, trainee quantity surveyor*

'I saw no point in doing a subject of no relevance to a career and getting drunk for three years! I wanted to get a life and earn my living.'

*Kieri White, RAF officer*

You can read their individual accounts in Chapters eight to seventeen.

# Chapter two

## Which jobs are available?

If you restricted your career choice to the jobs for which level 3 qualifications are *required* you would be ignoring the trends of the past few years and be limiting yourself to a narrow range of careers. The trend nowadays, for graduates to take more and more of the jobs that were previously taken by level 3 leavers, also means that 18-year-old leavers are now to be found in jobs previously done by GCSE/S grade leavers. This may be either because the competition is more severe and the employer can select from well-qualified applicants, or because the job itself has become more complex.

# The changing nature of jobs

Twenty years ago you could become a weights and measures inspector with a few GCSEs/S grades. Now, they are known as 'trading standards officers' and have degrees or degree-level qualifications – since they have to be knowledgeable not only about the technicalities of modern equipment for weighing and measuring, but also about the complexities of general consumer protection legislation, which has increased considerably in the same period. (There is a route, however, for people with level 3 qualifications if they first qualify as consumer advisers.)

Similarly, journalism was once entered largely by school-leavers with GCSEs or A levels. Now, the larger proportion of new entrants are graduates. Law has become practically an all-graduate profession (except for qualified legal executives who may enter with lower qualifications). Fifteen or twenty years ago it was usual for accountants and surveyors to train wholly in employment. Now graduate-entry routes are more common.

It will be interesting to see whether the increasing cost of full-time higher education – with variable top-up tuition fees in the pipeline – will, despite government hopes to the contrary, cause a reduction in numbers of students choosing full-time higher education. And if so, whether this will cause a knock-on effect and encourage more employers to introduce 18+ training programmes. Many are already recruiting people with level 3 qualifications and putting them through Apprenticeship programmes. (See Chapter five.)

New technology has meant new jobs appearing, as well as others disappearing over the years. Computer technology, for example, has led to a decrease in much administrative and draughting work once done manually, and to an increase in jobs associated with computer design and also with the use of computers. But who, 20 years ago, had heard of the job of a website designer or helpdesk technician? Other new jobs have appeared – for example, Connexions service personal adviser, call-centre worker, some jobs in complementary medicine and consumer adviser (mentioned above).

## Need for flexibility

Being too rigid in the definition of a level 3 job and thinking 'I'm not going for that. I could have applied with GCSEs' would be turning a blind eye to the practicalities. Police work, for example, now attracts more and more level 3 and graduate entrants each year. Level 3 qualifications are no longer solely associated with professional-level jobs. Many people who have them are in the Armed Forces in the ranks, rather than as officers, for example, gunners in the RAF Regiment or clerks in personnel and administration. They are found as administrative officers (junior clerical level) in the Civil Service as well as in local government and other office jobs. Some engineering companies are recruiting them to train first as technicians and then, if they wish to progress further, through the part-time Higher National level route, to become *incorporated engineers*.

Many jobs that do not stipulate the possession of level 3 qualifications, but are nevertheless entered by increasing numbers of level 3 leavers, offer very satisfying careers. They should not be automatically dismissed because the careers books state a lower minimum entry requirement. Emma Turner (see page 100), for example, joined the Inland Revenue first as a temporary employee then as a permanent member of staff at a level of job requiring GCSE passes. Six years on she is doing a job often done by people with degrees. In some cases you can enter at a slightly higher level or find that your qualifications exempt you from doing some of the exams you might have to take while training. Tom Lengthorn (see page 186) found that his National Diploma shortened his training period and permitted him to enrol immediately on a Higher National Certificate course, sponsored by his employer.

## Careers with minimum entry requirements of GCSEs/S grades, but which have a large number of entrants with level 3 qualifications

Airline pilot

Banking

Building society work

Civil Service administration

Court administration

Estate agency work

Health Service administration

Journalism

Laboratory technology

Legal executive work

Local government

Retail management

Technician work (architectural, engineering, planning, telecommunications)

# Why should employers value your qualifications?

Largely because, through having obtained advanced qualifications, you have demonstrated that you are:

- intelligent
- able to assimilate – and use – new information
- able to reason and analyse
- able to think for yourself
- capable of following further study and training.

Some jobs do want your subject knowledge. Some careers are possible only if you have passes in particular subjects. These are usually sciences. Scientific laboratory work and engineering come into this category, as do some kinds of surveying and some jobs in the construction industry (the lists that follow on pages 27-30 will demonstrate this).

Other careers are open to people with passes in any subject. In these areas employers are looking for the skills you have learned through advanced study, such as proficiency in:

- research
- analysis
- communication
- planning and managing your time.

You may also, through planning and carrying out projects and field work or through holding positions of responsibility at school or college, have learned valuable skills in working with other people, such as teamwork and leadership.

# A look at the jobs available

It can be very difficult to obtain accurate information, and many 18-year-olds feel that they simply do not know what sorts of jobs they can enter. Entry qualifications to careers are also constantly changing, as is the level of competition for each job.

Parents may not be able to help much because a lot of their information can be out of date. When they were at school, A levels had a rarity value and a higher currency for job-hunting than they have today. Then, they would provide an entry to more of the professions, and you could find that your parents are not too impressed to find that their son or daughter is considering careers that could previously have been entered with GCSEs/ S grades! They may also feel that they have given you the chance to stay at school or college until 18, and want to see more positive results in terms of improved career opportunities. Well meant as they are, these pressures are not always helpful.

So, applying for work and making the best use of qualifications require careful preparation and a lot of information and effort, particularly in areas of unemployment.

## Four job groups

It will be helpful to look at the jobs that may be available to you in groups based on the kind of subjects you have been taking. Note that the jobs listed include some that do not require level 3 qualifications as the minimum requirement, but which are taken up by significant numbers of students who hold them.

Jobs are divided into four categories. None of these categories includes jobs for which a full-time training course is the only route in. For example, nursing is not included because it is no longer possible to train on a salaried basis (although student nurses do receive bursaries from the NHS, and experienced healthcare assistants may be sponsored through the full-time diploma course on salary by their NHS Trusts).

**The four groups of jobs are:**

**Group 1** Science-based jobs that require at least one science subject at A level/H grade OR an appropriate National Diploma plus a range of GCSEs/S grades at A*-C/1-3, particularly mathematics and English language.

**Group 2** Technical jobs for which mathematics and at least one other science subject, often physics, are required at GCSE/S grade – and for which employers may also prefer some study of science at advanced level.

**Group 3** Jobs open to entrants with any level 3 qualification, but for which GCSE/S grade passes in English language and mathematics are required.

**Group 4** Jobs open to entrants with any level 3 qualification, but for which GCSEs/S grades would normally include English language.

## The importance of GCSEs and S grades

For people with no advanced-level science qualification, the range of subjects they have passed at GCSE/S grade can make a big difference to the opportunities open to them. It is therefore very important to try to ensure that you have at least English language and mathematics. Similarly, another science subject could open up many more careers, in areas such as surveying and technical marketing, and could increase your chances of a job in many others.

If your level 3 qualifications are in science subjects, employers may be looking for evidence of literacy and good all-round education, and so will be interested in English language and other humanities subjects studied at GCSE/S grade or AS level, including foreign languages.

## Subject preferences at level 3

It is unusual for employers to ask for specific humanities subjects, such as history or English literature. On the other hand, if the job needs a pass in a science subject, a requirement for chemistry, physics or both may be stated quite specifically.

Although academic qualifications are important for jobs (for some more than others), they are just one of the factors an employer will be looking at during the selection procedure. Finding someone who has the right personality and can fit in with existing staff may be more important to some employers than strings of academic qualifications. If a job requires a high level of verbal skill, an employer will give preference to someone who can demonstrate this, as well as other qualities for the job. These other skills are unlikely to be specified in terms of particular subjects, but will be judged through application forms and interviews. Recruitment and selection methods will be looked at in Chapter four.

## How to use the group lists

Although the list in Group 4 appears very long, don't forget that the groupings are based on minimum qualifications, and extra subjects such as mathematics and sciences can be an advantage in many of them. It follows that those who are qualified to seek jobs in Group 1 will, in most cases, also be qualified for jobs in Group 2. Those who would qualify for jobs in Group 2 are also likely to be qualified for those in Group 3. Retail trade, accountancy, legal work and many other careers welcome applicants with science subjects as well as those with humanities subjects.

Please remember that the lists that follow are only a rough guide and that entry requirements for some jobs will vary a great deal from company to company.

Lists have not been compiled for students on National Diploma courses since they generally have a fair idea of the range of jobs their qualifications will lead to. If, however, you are on such a course but are now wondering about entering a different career area, you should find some new ideas in Groups 3 and 4, and possibly in Group 2. People can and do use National Diplomas and other specialist level 3 qualifications to enter unrelated careers. Two such examples are Darren Fagan (page 139) and Phillip Mann (page 202).

## Find your group

**(i)** Are you taking science subjects, including physics, chemistry or general science?

No. Go to **question (ii)**

Yes

## Group 1 jobs

Airline pilot*

Engineering technician/technologist

Food science technician/technologist

Laboratory technician/technologist

Materials technician/technologist

Medical technician/technologist

Merchant Navy engineering officer

Non-destructive testing technician

Quality controller

*Entry is possible with lower qualifications, but if you hoped to be sponsored through training by an airline you would often find A levels in maths and/or physics required.*

Now look at **Group 2** jobs. You will be qualified for these too.

**(ii)** Are you taking humanities or social science subjects, and have a range of GCSEs/S grades including maths and physical or double integrated science at A*-C/1-3?

No. Go to **question (iii)**

Yes

## Group 2 jobs

Air traffic controller

Architectural technician/technologist

Army technician

Construction/building technician

Construction manager

Dispensing optician

IT helpdesk adviser

Medical photographer

Merchant Navy deck officer

Quantity surveyor

RAF technician

Royal Navy technician

Telecommunications technician

Now look at **Group 3** jobs. You will be qualified for these too.

**(iii)** Are you studying humanities or social science subjects and have maths at GCSE/S grade A*-C/1-3?

No. Go to **(iv)**

Yes

## Group 3 jobs

Accountant

Accounting technician

Actuary*

Administrative officer/assistant

Army officer

Auctioneer

Bank officer/management trainee

Barristers'/Advocates' clerk

Building society officer/management trainee

Building surveyor

Buyer/purchasing officer

Computer operator/programmer

Diplomatic Service officer

Financial services adviser

Market researcher

RAF officer

Royal Navy/Royal Marines officer

Stockbroker/equity salesperson

Surveyor, general practice

Taxation technician

Trading standards officer

Transport manager

*Although science passes are not necessary, maths at A level/H grade is required.*

Now look at **Group 4** jobs. You will be qualified for these too.

**(iv)** If you are studying humanities or social science subjects and have no maths or science GCSEs/S grades at A*-C/1-3, start here. BUT, please note that maths is required by the majority of employers in most career areas.

## Group 4 jobs

Advertising worker

Air cabin crew

Airline/airport administrator

Ambulance paramedic

Ambulance technician

Armed Forces (non-commissioned)

Business administrator

Civil Service, junior manager/administrative officer

Connexions service personal adviser

Consumer adviser

Customs and Excise officer

Estate agent

Fast food-outlet manager

Firefighter

Freight forwarder

Hospitality manager

Housing officer/manager

Insurance broker

Insurance claims official

Insurance technician

Insurance underwriter (normally beginning as an insurance technician)

Journalist (broadcast or print)

Legal executive

Leisure centre manager/sport-related work

Library assistant

Local government administrator

Marketing executive/assistant

Market researcher

Photographer

Planning support worker

Police officer

Retail manager

Sales executive

Tourist information centre assistant

Travel agent

## Different employer requirements

There are many jobs that do not fit precisely into any one of these fairly loose groupings.

Different employers have different requirements in terms of qualifications. For example, retail management is listed in Group 4 because many stores will take suitable candidates with any level 3 qualifications. However, most ask specifically for GCSE/S grade mathematics. You will see that that each job has been grouped by minimum entry qualification. Some employers may demand higher grades in certain subjects. The above is only a very general guide.

Entry and training information for the careers that have been listed follow in this chapter. For more detailed information (particularly on those careers that are not featured in the career profiles later in this book), consult the resources recommended in Chapter seven, such as the KUDOS or KeyCLIPS databases, which may be available at your school, college or the local office of your Connexions/careers service.

# Career entry and training in brief

## Accountant

Many companies in industry and commerce, as well as local authorities and the Civil Service, recruit and train accountants. Trainees study for the examinations of one of the accountancy professional bodies while training – Chartered Association of Certified Accountants (ACCA), Chartered Institute of Management Accountants (CIMA), Chartered Institute of Public and Finance Accountancy (CIPFA), Institutes of Chartered Accountants (ICAEW, ICAS and ICAI). Policy on giving day-release varies. Some employers expect trainees to take evening classes.

Availability – nationwide.

## Accounting technician

Recruitment is carried out by the same types of employer as above. The minimum entry requirement is at GCSE/S grade, although many entrants have higher qualifications. Trainees may study for the examinations of the Association of Accounting Technicians (AAT) or of the ACCA. It is possible to move on to professional accountancy training after qualifying.

Availability – nationwide.

See the career profile of Fiona Catling (page 144).

## Actuary

Actuaries are employed by insurance companies, pensions companies, other financial institutions and some government departments. It is more usual to enter this career after a degree course – 95% of entrants are graduates – but entry with level 3 qualifications is still possible provided that they include a good A level/H grade in maths. Trainees study for the examinations of the Faculty and Institute of Actuaries and normally take between three and six years.

Availability – nationwide – but more likely in cities where large financial institutions are based.

## Administrative officer/assistant (sometimes known as clerical worker)

The minimum entry requirement is at GCSE/S grade, although many entrants have level 3 qualifications. Many employers give day release for Edexcel BTEC/SQA qualifications.

Availability – nationwide.

## Advertising worker

There is no standard route into advertising. Advertising agencies say academic qualifications are not essential, yet the majority of entrants are graduates. Students with level 3 qualifications are sometimes able to work their way up from junior positions. Trainees may attend courses run by the Institute of Practitioners in Advertising, or the Communications, Advertising and Marketing Foundation.

Availability – limited geographically. Most work is in cities, with a concentration of employers in London.

See the career profile of Sam Myers (page 125).

## Air cabin crew

Training is carried out on the job by the employing airline. The minimum entry requirement is at GCSE/S grade, although many entrants have level 3 qualifications. The minimum age is normally 20, following experience in a job dealing with the public, but this varies. Airlines have different requirements regarding height, eyesight and previous experience.

Availability – staff must be able to reach their base airport within specified time limits. Mobility essential.

See the career profile of Eddy Tumath (page 225).

## Air traffic controller

Training varies according to airport owners, but all trainees must pass Civil Aviation Authority (CAA) exams. The most common entry route is as a National Air Traffic Services (NATS) cadet. Minimum entry qualifications are five GCSEs/S grades at A*-C/1-3, including English, maths and a science. NATS cadets must have studied for level 3 qualifications.

Availability – at airports. Mobility essential.

See the career profile of Henry Marshall (page 217).

## Airline/airport administrator

Staff work in general administration, marketing, selling, accounts, computing, customer relations, and so on, plus flight planning and scheduling. Training is as for the individual jobs in other companies. Flight operations staff often start in computing or administration.

Availability – limited geographically. Staff must live near airports or near airlines' head offices.

## Airline pilot

Training opportunities vary from year to year. Some airlines offer full or partial sponsorship to a flying school approved by the CAA – which is the only method of obtaining a commercial pilot's licence. Airlines normally ask for level 3 qualifications. It is also possible to qualify as a privately-funded student at a recognised flying school.

Entry qualifications may be lower.

Availability – only at specified schools. In some years no recruitment is undertaken.

## Ambulance paramedic

Paramedics must have qualified and worked for 12 months as ambulance technicians and pass an entry examination before they can be considered for training. Training is on the job with attendance at training centres.

Availability – nationwide.

## Ambulance technician

Training is carried out by the employing ambulance trust. There are no national minimum entry requirements but some services ask for two A levels/H grades or equivalent.

Availability – nationwide.

## Architectural technician/technologist

Technicians are employed by architects' practices, construction companies and local authorities to work as members of design teams under the supervision of qualified architects. Part-time study usually leads to BTEC/SQA National and Higher National qualifications. The minimum entry requirement is GCSEs/S grades, although some entrants have level 3 qualifications. Members of the British Institute of Architectural Technologists are known as technologists. Non-members may be known as either technologists or technicians.

Availability – nationwide.

## Armed Forces (non-commissioned)

A wide variety of jobs, known as trades or categories, is available. Specific GCSEs/S grades are required for some. Training leads to nationally-recognised qualifications (e.g. City and Guilds) where appropriate. You can obtain information from your nearest Armed Forces careers information office. In some of the more popular trades, entrants often have level 3 qualifications.

Availability – nationwide. Mobility essential.

## Army officer

Entrants with level 3 qualifications may apply to join at officer level. Science subjects are required for entry to technical branches. You can obtain information from your nearest Armed Forces careers information office.

Availability – nationwide. Mobility essential.

## Army technician

The entry level is GCSEs/S grades at A*-C/1-3 in appropriate subjects, but candidates with higher qualifications sometimes apply. You can obtain information from your nearest Armed Forces careers information office. Training can lead to nationally-recognised qualifications.

Availability – nationwide. Mobility essential.

## Auctioneer

It is possible to become an auctioneer without any qualifications, although many entrants have level 2 or 3 qualifications and many employers expect trainees to take professional examinations. Trainees may study for the examinations of the Royal Institution of Chartered Surveyors.

Availability – nationwide.

## Bank officer/management trainee

All the high street banks recruit trainees. It is advisable to study for the professional exams run by the Institute of Financial Services or the Chartered Institute of Bankers in Scotland for promotion.

Availability – nationwide, but it may be necessary to agree to travel daily to any branch within a limited geographical area.

See the career profile of Darren Fagan (page 139).

## Barristers'/Advocates' clerks

Barristers'/Advocates' clerks deal with the administration in barristers' chambers (advocates' stables in Scotland). They liaise between solicitors, clients and their barristers/advocates, make appointments, collect fees and do routine administrative tasks. A major responsibility is bringing in work for their barristers/advocates – which they do mainly by keeping in contact with solicitors. Senior clerks are also responsible for allocating cases to barristers/advocates, negotiating fees and managing the chambers'/stables' finances. The usual minimum entry requirements for barristers' clerks are four GCSEs, grades A*-C, including English and maths. Many entrants have higher qualifications. Advocates' clerks need H grade English and evidence of numeracy.

Availability – mainly in London and Edinburgh and in other cities where there are law courts.

## Building society officer/management trainee

Some of the larger societies recruit trainees. Not all take 18-year-old entrants. It is advisable to study for the Institute of Financial Services/ Chartered Institute of Bankers in Scotland examinations, which now cover building society work, for promotion.

Availability – nationwide, but it may be necessary to agree to travel daily to any branch within a limited geographical area.

See the career profile of Will McAlpine (page 135).

## Building surveyor

Some trainee positions exist with local authorities, the Civil Service and private construction companies. However, although both a part-time and distance-learning route to qualification still exist, it is becoming more usual to enter the profession with a degree. Some major employers are willing to sponsor students through degree courses.

Availability – nationwide.

See the career profile of Matthew Morfoot (page 206).

## Business administrator

Some employers run training schemes for entrants with level 3 qualifications and give on-the-job training, plus the opportunity to gain BTEC/SQA Higher Certificates.

Availability – it may be necessary to leave your home area to find a suitable scheme.

See the career profile of Fiona King, page 91.

## Buyer/purchasing officer

Purchasing officers work in industry, commerce, local authorities, the Civil Service and the National Health Service. Their counterpart in retailing is the buyer. Companies may recruit students with level 3 qualifications for direct entry to purchasing schemes, or may first put them through general management training. Training normally includes part-time study (often through evening classes), leading to the examinations of the Chartered Institute of Purchasing and Supply.

Availability – nationwide.

## Civil Service, junior manager/administrative officer

All departments (e.g. Work and Pensions, HM Revenue and Customs, Ministry of Defence) recruit school and college leavers.

Availability – nationwide, but the opportunity to work for a specific department depends on where you live. Junior managers are expected to be mobile.

See the career profiles of Melanie Helps (page 93) and Emma Turner (page 100).

## Computer operator/programmer

There are training possibilities with some large computer users and in the Civil Service and local authorities. It may be possible to find a position as a trainee programmer, but many entrants with level 3 qualifications begin as computer operators. Training is on the job, but some employers encourage trainees to study for BTEC/SQA qualifications or the examinations of the British Computer Society.

Availability – nationwide.

## Connexions service personal adviser

Personal advisers support and help young people in the decisions they have to make regarding education, careers, training and personal development. They may also help them with problems regarding health, lifestyle, housing, financial support and personal issues. Qualification is through a national training programme, which leads to a diploma.

Availability – nationwide.

See the career profile of Tamarin Gibbs (page 111).

## Construction/building technician

Technicians can have one of several roles. They may work as building technicians, drawing up plans and supervising on site; as estimators, costing projects and producing estimates; or even specialise in buying. Minimum entry requirements are normally four GCSEs at grades A*-C or equivalent, but some employers may recruit young people with level 3 qualifications who can begin working for HNC/HND/NVQ levels 3, 4.

Availability – nationwide.

## Construction manager

Many of the large construction companies recruit trainees. Trainees take a two-year Higher National Certificate in building studies on day release, followed, after some experience, by the professional examinations of the Chartered Institute of Building.

Availability – depends on where you live. Large companies may assist with accommodation if you have to leave your home area.

See career profile of Tom Winter (page 199).

## Consumer adviser

Consumer advisers work in Trading Standards departments, advising the public on aspects of legislation regarding the buying and selling of goods and services and consumer rights, but without having the specialist and in-depth knowledge of trading standards officers. If they successfully complete the Diploma in Consumer Affairs, they may apply to become trading standards officers.

## Customs and Excise officer

There are opportunities to work at ports, airports and in VAT offices. Entry is into Civil Service grades. Most executive officers begin in VAT work.

Availability – nationwide.

## Diplomatic Service officer

Diplomatic Service staff protect and promote British interests abroad.

Availability – in Britain, only in London; otherwise, worldwide. Officers are expected to be mobile.

See the career profile of Anna Bantin (page 103).

## Dispensing optician

The minimum entry requirement is five GCSEs/S grades at A*-C/1-3, including English, maths and a science, although many entrants have level 3 qualifications. Trainees learn to fit and supply optical appliances, working to a prescription. Trainees must study for the examinations of the Association of Dispensing Opticians. Study takes three years through day release or distance learning.

Availability – nationwide.

See the career profile of Sarah Goodridge (page 192).

## Engineering technician/technologist

Engineering technicians undertake design, planning, testing, product development or laboratory work under the supervision of professional engineers. Some employers recruit entrants with level 3 qualifications. Some may give preference to holders of advanced vocational qualifications.

Availability – increasing. You may have to leave your home area in order to find an employer in a particular branch of engineering.

See the career profile of Samantha Hubbard (page 183).

## Estate agent

There are no minimum entry requirements, but many entrants have level 3 qualifications. Training varies according to employer. Many expect trainees to qualify for membership of either the National Association of Estate Agents or the Royal Institution of Chartered Surveyors.

Availability – nationwide.

See the career profile of Phillip Mann (page 202).

## Fast food-outlet manager

At least one of the major chains offers a training scheme leading to restaurant management. Progress is at a trainee's own speed.

Availability – nationwide.

See the career profile of Jake Harris (page 117).

## Financial services adviser

They give advice on all kinds of financial 'products', including insurance, pensions, mortgages and investments. Some are employed by organisations such as banks or insurance companies (see the career profiles of Phillip Mann on page 202 and Will McAlpine on page 135 – both mention referring their clients on to a financial adviser). Others work for firms of independent financial advisers. It is necessary to pass professional examinations.

Availability – nationwide.

See the career profile of Justin Randall (page 147).

## Firefighter

There are no standard minimum entry requirements, but each Fire Service may set its own. Basic training takes between 12 and 16 weeks.

Availability – nationwide.

## Food science technician/technologist

There are openings to work in food analysis, testing and quality control with a wide variety of food manufacturers, in the Civil Service, with supermarket chains and in some university and college laboratories. Many employers prefer graduates, but some have openings for entrants with level 3 qualifications. Trainees may study for a Higher National Certificate in food science/technology.

Availability – nationwide.

## Freight forwarder

Freight forwarders are responsible for organising the movement of goods. They book transport cargo space, using the most suitable and cost-effective route, taking into account factors like the perishable nature of the goods, cost, travel time and security.

Availability – nationwide.

## Hospitality manager

Managers run hotels and other hospitality outlets or departments within them – such as front of house, accommodation services, food and beverages or housekeeping. Some large hotels and chains offer management training schemes and/or Advanced Apprenticeships.

Availability – nationwide.

See the career profile of Louise Matson (page 128).

## Housing officer/manager

There are opportunities with local authorities and housing associations as well as in the private rented sector. It is useful to have the Institute of Housing's professional diploma for promotion. The usual route for students with level 3 qualifications is to find a trainee position and study part-time for a BTEC Higher National Certificate in housing studies, followed by two years' study for the professional diploma.

Availability – nationwide.

See the career profile of Linda Brockwell (page 107).

## Human resources (personnel) manager

Opportunities exist in every kind of industrial, commercial and public sector organisation. Some employers train students with level 3 qualifications directly for personnel work. The majority prefer them first to complete a general management training scheme or gain administrative experience. It is helpful to study for the examinations of the Chartered Institute of Personnel and Development.

Availability – nationwide.

## IT helpdesk adviser

Most students with level 3 qualifications start as IT trainees and learn their duties on the job. They are trained by senior colleagues to give technical support to customers or colleagues with IT problems, such as advice on suitable software to purchase, type of printer to use, amount of memory needed, and tips and techniques on how to get the most from the equipment. It is usual also to attend short technical courses.

Availability – nationwide.

## Insurance broker

Brokers are independent advisers who act as the link between client and insurer. They arrange suitable insurance cover with a company, negotiate a fee and charge the client a fee for setting up the policy.

Availability – nationwide.

## Insurance claims official

Claims officials look at all the information that comes in from a client who is making a claim. They may need to ask for more detail or request specialist reports. They are usually authorised to accept claims up to a certain value and refer more complicated or expensive claims to a manager.

Availability – nationwide, but only in towns or cities where insurance companies are based.

## Insurance technician

Technicians do clerical and administrative work in support of more senior staff – brokers, underwriters, etc.

Availability – nationwide, but only in towns or cities where insurance companies are based.

## Insurance underwriter

Underwriters assess the degree of risk involved in offering cover to individual clients. They weigh up all the facts, and decide whether to issue the policy on behalf of their company and what to charge. Large companies run training programmes for each of the three jobs above – and it is normal for non-graduates to train first in one of them before moving into underwriting work. Smaller companies may recruit to fill specific jobs. It is advisable to study for the examinations of the Chartered Insurance Institute for promotion.

Availability – usually in large towns.

## Journalist (broadcast)

The BBC runs a news trainee scheme (not every year) for people who wish to work in (or begin in) regional broadcasting. Many successful national names started in the regions, including journalist Kate Adie and news presenter George Alagiah. You can check on the website (www.bbc.co.uk/jobs) to find out when the scheme will next be running.

## Journalist (print)

There is no standard entry requirement, but most editors have a working minimum of five GCSEs/S grades at A*-C/1-3, including English. In practice, many entrants have degrees. Some regional newspaper groups run training schemes for students with level 3 qualifications, which include sponsorship to courses approved by the National Council for the Training of Journalists.

Availability – nationwide.

## Laboratory technician/technologist

Opportunities exist with industrial companies, in universities, colleges and schools and in the public sector. Work may be in pharmaceuticals, cosmetics, food and drink manufacture, utilities, health research, etc. Training normally includes day release for a Higher National Certificate in applied biology, chemistry or biochemistry.

Availability – nationwide.

See the career profile of Greg Rogers (page 189).

## Legal executive (England and Wales)

The minimum entry qualification is at GCSE/S grade, but many entrants have higher qualifications. Opportunities exist with firms of solicitors and with local authorities. Small firms are unlikely to take trainees. Part-time study leads to the examinations of the Institute of Legal Executives. Fully-qualified legal executives may become trainee solicitors.

Availability – nationwide. There is no exact equivalent in Scotland, although many legal firms employ assistants who do similar work.

See the career profile of Lyndsey Taggart (page 159).

## Leisure centre manager/sport-related work

There are opportunities with local authorities, sports clubs and commercial leisure and fitness centres, sometimes attached to hotels. It is not essential to take further examinations but many entrants study for a Higher National Certificate in leisure studies and for membership of the Institute of Leisure and Amenity Management.

Availability – nationwide.

See the career profile of Craig Cotterill (page 132).

## Library assistant

Opportunities exist in public libraries run by local authorities and in some large organisations that have specialist libraries. Training is on the job. It is not possible to become a chartered librarian without taking a full-time degree course.

Availability – nationwide.

See the career profile of Lindsay Currie (page 121).

## Local government administrator

Very few local authorities now run training schemes specifically for holders of level 3 qualifications. However, many students enter the clerical grades and gain promotion. Training usually includes day release for BTEC/SQA National qualifications in public administration or business studies.

Availability – nationwide.

## Marketing executive/assistant

Opportunities exist with many manufacturing companies and providers of services. It is not usual to start in marketing straight from school, but rather to join a company's marketing department at the end of a commercial management training scheme or after gaining administrative experience. Training is on the job, but people may choose to study for Institute of Marketing diplomas.

Availability – nationwide.

See the career profile of Sarah Gallimore (page 171).

## Market researcher

Market research is a largely graduate occupation. Students with level 3 qualifications may, however, find openings. Training is largely on the job, but people may choose to study for the Market Research Society's diploma.

Availability – mainly limited to large cities.

## Materials technician/technologist

Materials technicians investigate the properties of materials to make sure that the products they are used in will be safe, reliable and efficient. The minimum entry qualification is usually a relevant level 3 qualification.

Training is carried out by employers, often through an Apprenticeship programme. Technicians may study through distance-learning programmes organised by the Institute of Materials. Many proceed to degree-level study.

Availability – nationwide.

## Medical photographer

Some hospitals – usually the larger ones – and medical research establishments have a specialist medical photography department. Staff make records of operations and particular cases and illustrate teaching material. The minimum entry requirement is at GCSE/S grade, although many entrants have level 3 qualifications. Training is carried out on the job, supplemented by part-time study for the qualifications of the British Institute of Professional Photography.

Availability – nationwide, but vacancies infrequent.

## Medical technician/technologist

Trainees are employed in the laboratories of NHS Hospital Trusts, and sometimes in forensic laboratories and labs owned by pharmaceutical companies and government research departments. Training is normally given on the job and S/NVQs are available. Day release for study to Higher National Certificate level may be given. However, promotion to medical biochemist would require a degree course.

Availability – nationwide.

## Merchant Navy deck officer

Several British shipping companies recruit students with level 3 qualifications to train as deck or navigating officers. Work may be on passenger or cargo ships. Alternate periods of training are spent at sea and at college studying for a foundation degree.

Availability – nationwide. Mobility essential.

See the career profile of Jo Cox (page 221).

## Merchant Navy engineering officer

As above.

## Non-destructive testing technician

Non-destructive testing (NDT) is a branch of engineering concerned with the methods of detecting and evaluating flaws in materials – without in any way harming the material or structure being tested. A qualification in materials is essential for entry to this work. (See Materials technician/technologist entry.) Non-destructive testing methods are used across a wide range of industries.

Availability – nationwide.

## Personnel manager – see Human resources manager

## Photographer

The minimum entry requirement is at GCSE/S grade level, although many entrants have level 3 qualifications. Starting as a junior in a studio and studying for the examinations of the British Institute of Professional Photography is perfectly possible, but vacancies may be hard to find. Editors of some newspapers recruit trainee press photographers and sponsor them through training courses approved by the National Council for the Training of Journalists.

Availability – nationwide, but travel may be necessary to find a suitable opening.

See the career profile of Rob Wilson (page 115).

## Planning support worker

The minimum entry requirement is at GCSE/S grade, although many entrants have level 3 qualifications. Planning support staff, which may include planning enforcement staff, planning administrators and technical support staff, work under the supervision of qualified planners. Most training opportunities are in local authorities' planning departments, although technicians are also employed in private sector planning practices. Technicians usually work towards NVQ/SVQ level 3 in town planning support. It is possible to become a professional planner after further study.

Availability – nationwide.

## Police officer

There are no national minimum entry requirements. Each individual police force sets its own. Many entrants have level 3 qualifications. The minimum age of entry is 18-and-a-half, and although some people join straight from school or college, many get some alternative work experience first. Training is all done internally.

Availability – nationwide, but it may be necessary to leave home if your local constabulary is not recruiting.

See the career profile of Heidi Schulz (page 155).

## Quality controller

Quality controllers conduct tests at various stages of manufacture and analyse them afterwards. Some tests may be simple visual checks; others involve the use of laboratory equipment. Entry requirements to this work vary, but people with level 3 qualifications are often recruited in industries that use complex laboratory equipment.

Availability – nationwide.

## Quantity surveyor

Quantity surveyors manage the financial side of building and civil engineering projects. The main route to qualification is to take a degree course accredited by either the Royal Institution of Chartered Surveyors or the Chartered Institute of Building. This may be done on a part-time basis. It is also possible to begin by taking a Higher National Diploma or foundation degree course before proceeding to an honours degree.

Availability – nationwide.

See the career profile of Matthew Morfoot (page 206).

## RAF officer

Entrants with level 3 qualifications may apply for entry at officer level. Science subjects are required for entry to technical branches. You can obtain information from your nearest Armed Forces careers information office.

Availability – nationwide. Mobility essential.

## RAF technician

The entry level is GCSEs/S grades at A*-C/1-3 in appropriate subjects, but candidates with higher qualifications sometimes apply. You can obtain information from your nearest Armed Forces careers information office. Training can lead to nationally-recognised qualifications.

Availability – nationwide. Mobility essential.

See the career profile of Kieri White (page 165).

## Retail manager

Some, but not all, companies run training schemes. Training is usually internal with no professional exams to take.

Availability – nationwide. Mobility essential. Companies normally assist with accommodation costs.

See the career profiles of Kirk Armitt (page 173) and Gemma Wright (page 178).

## Royal Navy/Royal Marines officer

Entrants with level 3 qualifications may apply to enter at officer level. Science subjects are required for entry to technical branches of the Royal Navy. You can obtain information from your nearest Armed Forces careers information office. See also 'Royal Navy technician' below.

Availability – nationwide. Mobility essential.

## Royal Navy technician

The entry level is GCSEs/S grades at A*-C/1-3 in appropriate subjects, but candidates with higher qualifications sometimes apply. Training can lead to nationally-recognised qualifications. You can obtain information from your nearest Armed Forces careers information office.

Availability – nationwide. Mobility essential.

## Sales executive

There are opportunities in the manufacturing industry and in advertisement sales for publications. A few students with level 3 qualifications find jobs in sales straight from school. The majority join a company in another capacity and move into the sales department. Training is on the job.

Availability – nationwide.

## Stockbroker/equity salesperson

There are no minimum entry requirements, but many entrants now have degrees. Students with level 3 qualifications are also recruited, but the annual number of openings is small. Training is on the job, with compulsory examinations to be taken before salespeople may advise clients. Study is usually done in the trainee's own time.

Availability – limited geographically. Most work is in London, although there are also opportunities in large cities, mainly Belfast, Birmingham, Edinburgh, Glasgow, Leeds and Manchester.

## Surveyor, general practice

The main route to qualification is to take a degree course accredited by either the Royal Institution of Chartered Surveyors or the Chartered Institute of Building. This may be done on a part-time basis. It is also possible to begin by taking a Higher National Diploma or foundation degree course before proceeding to an honours degree. Some major employers are willing to sponsor students through degree courses.

Availability – nationwide, but depends on individual employers' preference for level 3 entrants or graduates.

## Taxation technician

Trainee positions exist with tax consultancy firms and accountancy practices. The minimum entry requirement is four GCSEs/S grades at A*-C/1-3 but employers often give preference to applicants with A levels or Highers in numerate subjects. Trainees study for the examinations of the Association of Taxation Technicians and may follow these with those of the Chartered Institute of Taxation.

Availability – nationwide.

## Telecommunications technician

There are openings with one or two companies that train entrants with level 3 qualifications. Training is a combination of theory and practice on site, and normally includes Higher National level qualifications.

Availability – national.

See the career profile of Lee Irwin (page 196).

## Tourist information centre assistant

Minimum entry standard is usually four GCSEs/S grades at A*-C/1-3, but many entrants have higher qualifications or previous relevant experience. Knowledge of languages is particularly useful. Training is mainly on the job, supplemented by attendance at short courses run by Tourist Boards.

Availability – in towns, cities and tourist areas. This is a popular job and vacancies do not arise very frequently.

There is no case study of a tourist information centre assistant – but see the profile of Gemma Lawson (page 213) for a description of a varied career in travel and tourism.

## Trading standards officer

The normal entry requirement is now a degree in consumer protection, but there is also an entry route for people who have previously worked as consumer advisers and have obtained the Trading Standards Institute's Diploma in Consumer Affairs. People with level 3 qualifications may be able to find openings at this level.

Availability – nationwide.

## Transport manager

There are openings with road passenger transport companies, train operating companies and with shipping and ferry companies. Some large firms run their own management training schemes. Training is on the job, although trainees may be encouraged to take the examinations of the Chartered Institute of Transport.

Availability – limited geographically.

## Travel agent

Most travel agencies recruit at GCSE/S grade or through work-based training. However, older applicants with higher qualifications are often accepted. Training is mainly on the job with part-time or distance-learning study for NVQs/SVQs in travel services. The larger groups run short courses at their own training centres.

Availability – nationwide.

There is no case study of a travel agent – but see Gemma Lawson (page 213) for a description of a varied career in travel and tourism.

# Chapter three

## Job-hunting

It has already been suggested that job-hunting is not easy. How do you find out about jobs – where they are, and what they involve? There can be differences in the qualifications required by different employers for very similar jobs. How do you know which employers are likely to have suitable openings and how do you hear about vacancies? If employment prospects are poor in your neighbourhood, would it be worthwhile trying further afield? How much choice will you have in a larger organisation about where you work, and will you be able to afford to live away from home?

There are several sources of help available to you.

# Sources of help

## Connexions/careers services

A very good starting point is to talk to the personal/careers adviser from your local Connexions/careers centre. A central part of a personal/careers adviser's work is to get to know local industry and employers. He or she will therefore be able to make suggestions of suitable local firms to approach. These could be employers who regularly take leavers with level 3 qualifications, employers who occasionally take them, or even some who do not usually employ them but are operating in an area of work that interests you and who may therefore be worth contacting. You might be able to persuade such an employer to take you on. Many Connexions/careers services produce lists of employers in their area with suitable training schemes. Some post them on their websites. Find out the address of their local website – log on and keep looking!

You should get the website address from your personal/careers adviser, but if you haven't met one yet you can go to:

- www.connexions-direct.com (click on local services)
- www.careersserviceni.com (Northern Ireland)
- www.careers-scotland.org.uk
- www.careerswales.com

and find your local office from there.

## Further afield

In the same way that your personal/careers advisers and careers teachers know local industry, there are advisers in every other part of the country who know about other job vacancies. They will have placed their own job information on the internet. Again, go to the main Connexions/careers services sites and identify an area. Then search.

Sometimes it may be essential to start your career in London. It is very important to look at the economics of moving there. The starting salaries may seem high, but the cost of living is also high, and pay doesn't go far. So, you may need the help of friends or relatives who could offer accommodation until you have found your feet. Some employers may be willing to assist.

Once your personal/careers adviser has established what type of job you are looking for, he or she may arrange to notify you of any vacancies received at the Connexions/careers centre. But you should not let it rest there – use all the resources or help you can.

If you are at an independent school you will probably use the services of ISCO (Independent Schools Careers Organisation), which gives advice to pupils at member schools. You may also use the local Connexions/careers service.

## Careers publishers

### Hobsons

Hobsons is a publishing company that produces careers material. It publishes a very useful annual publication, *Job Book*, which lists the national and regional companies recruiting at various levels. It contains details of organisations that recruit leavers with level 3 qualifications and then offer training and the opportunity to take further qualifications. You will find information about companies and addresses to write to for further details and application forms. A new edition is produced every year. Schools and colleges should have a current copy.

The same company also provides Springboard Student Service. You may register with this to receive free careers information by email – including any from employers likely to be of interest to you. Log on to www. springboard.hobsons.co.uk and see what is there. (It's a free service.)

### Lifetime Publishing

The Student Helpbook series (of which this book is a part) from Lifetime Publishing also includes the titles *Excel at Interviews* and *CVs and Applications*, which are both of great help to jobseekers. Your school or college may have copies of these, as well as the videos *Choices @ 18* and *The Essential Interview Video*.

### Trotman Publishing

Specialist careers publisher, Trotman, in addition to producing a vast number of books on individual careers, also produces an annually-updated careers guide. Since the Connexions service nationally stopped publishing its hard copy annual guide this is the only one on the market that is always up to date. (Connexions does, though, have a website, which has a regularly-updated careers section jobs4u, at www.connexions-direct.com/jobs4u.)

## The internet

This is rapidly becoming a major source of information on:

- particular careers
- specific vacancies
- application and interview tips.

See Springboard and jobs4u above.

New websites are springing up daily. Many are aimed at experienced job seekers and are not appropriate for school and college leavers, but if you find the right one or two they could be very useful. Below are notes on some of the more suitable ones. You will find others as you browse!

- www.monster.co.uk

Easy-to-use site with information on a range of jobs, plus application and interview tips.

- www.fish4.co.uk

Large site. Very easy to use.

- www.leisurejobs.com

Jobs in leisure, sport and tourism throughout the UK.

- www.jobsgopublic.co.uk

This could be for you if you are looking for a job in the public sector. It includes health services, local authorities, police forces, etc. under occupational headings – e.g. administration, fire, health, housing, leisure, local government or police.

- www.LGcareers.com

This is local government's own website, run on behalf of all local authorities. It carries careers information and job advertisements at all levels from junior to very senior management. It also has career profiles of some unusual jobs like tree officer, committee administrator and land charges officer.

When you have identified the kind of job that you want, you can visit some individual employers' websites. (Not all employers have them.) Many can be reached through links from one of the above sites. You can request information packs and application forms online – and in many cases can even apply online.

Most professional associations and organisations also have websites. Where appropriate, details are given in the 'Addresses' and 'Further information' sections that follow each career profile.

## Advertisements

The local newspaper is a good source of information about vacancies in local companies. It is useful to start reading the job advertisements section regularly from the beginning of year 13. Although it may be too early to apply, the information gives you a feel for the job market. In areas of high unemployment it will be a depressingly quick exercise. But it is still helpful to keep your eye on the local job situation and get used to reading job advertisements. It is also worth looking in the industrial news section of the newspaper in case a new company is moving to your area. You will also see news of companies that are reducing staff or closing down. But, do remember, it can be possible for a company to be making older staff redundant while still recruiting young people.

Of the national newspapers the *Daily Telegraph* probably has the best range of jobs with level 3 qualifications. However, most vacancies in the national press are for experienced people, although there are a few seasonal vacancies for graduates and 18-year-old leavers. The specialist press also carries vacancies for experienced staff, but in some cases magazines such as *New Scientist* or *Leisure Manager* can be useful for job seekers with level 3 qualifications too.

Whatever the source, if the vacancies sound at all promising, write or phone for more details. Making enquiries does not commit you to an application, and making an application does not commit you to the job – even if it is offered to you.

## Temporary or part-time work

Don't overlook the opportunities provided by temporary jobs or even part-time jobs if you cannot find anything full time as soon as you leave school or college. These very often lead on to other opportunities in the same organisation, or can provide good experience for you. Some of the young people featured in the career profiles started in this way. Darren Fagan (see page 139) was offered a full-time job as an assistant manager because he had already done weekend and holiday work in a similar career area.

## Personal contact

Otherwise known as networking. Other useful sources of help might be teachers, friends, parents, aunts, uncles and other relatives who may have information about the companies they work for, or other openings heard about on the grapevine. You may have a Saturday job with a company that might be interested in employing you full time. Your Saturday boss may know of someone else who has a vacancy. It is always worth asking around.

## Professional associations

Some professional associations can help job seekers who are keen to get into a particular field of work. They usually have careers information on their websites, and in addition some publish lists of firms that recruit trainees.

# Making your own job

There is an alternative to looking for an employer, which is to create your own job and become your own boss. This is not easy for someone with no work experience, but it has been done. (See Chapter six on Enterprise.)

# Chapter four

## Applications and interviews

## Making approaches

Once you have a list of possible organisations, it is always worth approaching them directly. This could be done in November or December of year 13. If it is a large organisation, such as a bank or the Civil Service, you will probably find that they put information about specific job vacancies and application forms on their websites. You might be asked either:

- to download the application form, print it off and complete it in ink

- to complete it online.

Online applications are becoming more and more popular. Some companies in fact recruit no other way.

All this presupposes that you have access to the internet and have an email address. If not, you can probably use your school or college facilities. If you have left school or college, try your local library. Most of them offer internet services and will help you to set up an email address (for example with Yahoo!, which can be accessed from anywhere). There is usually no charge for this service – although you will need to be a library member, show your card and sign in on each visit. If you do not have a library card, you may still be able to use the computers as a visitor.

If there is nothing on the internet you should send a short letter asking for information and an application form. You could also include your curriculum vitae (CV).

# Speculative applications

Sending off lots of letters is both time consuming and costly, and in some cases it can produce a very poor return. Some employers may not even bother to reply, which is very depressing when you have taken a lot of trouble to write to them. It is not uncommon to hear stories of people writing 50 or so letters without receiving any replies. (Employers who haven't any intention of offering jobs get fed up with all the letters.) However, if one interview comes about as the result of your speculative applications it could lead to a job. Every year many leavers do get jobs this way, and it may be in your interest to try. It might save a lot of time and expense if you were to check your list of companies and organisations with your personal/careers adviser or careers teacher so as to eliminate the definite non-starters.

## What should a speculative letter contain?

- your name
- your age
- your qualifications
- what course you are doing at present
- where
- exams to be taken
- why you are interested in this type of work (briefly)
- details of any relevant work experience
- how and where you may be contacted.

End by saying you would appreciate being informed if they intend to recruit any trainees in this career area.

Tips

- Use plain, white, unlined writing paper.

- Use the correct forms of address and signature. Dear Sir/Dear Madam takes *Yours faithfully*. Dear Mr Smith takes *Yours sincerely*. These forms matter to a lot of recruiters.

- Keep it short. No-one has time to wade through lengthy letters. BUT don't miss out anything important!

# Writing a CV

A CV, or personal history, is something you will probably be encouraged to put together at school or college. You might have done so already in careers lessons, like Jake Wilks (page 209). If you haven't done this, it is a useful exercise because it makes you think seriously about how to approach employers and how to present the factors they will use in assessing applicants for interviews. There are some suggested models for a CV on the following pages, which could be a useful guide. Remember to include information about your activities outside school or college, such as your interests, hobbies, sports, social societies, cadets corps, Duke of Edinburgh Awards and so on, because employers are interested in these as well as in academic achievements and school activities. You should also add any other skills you have, such as IT, knowledge of computer packages, languages you are familiar with, or the possession of a driving licence.

It is a good idea to spend some time putting together a CV, so that it is ready should you be asked for a copy. It needs to be kept somewhere safe, or preferably on a disk, where it can be easily accessed, updated and printed off. Be sure to update it regularly. Many people already at work keep a CV, check it regularly and amend it every time they change jobs. As a student you will have a lot of relevant information in your Progress File. You can use this as a basis for writing a CV – but also, remember to take the file with you to interviews. Employers may wish to see it.

## Suggested formats for a CV

### CVs have changed!

There used to be one standard method of writing them – chronological. Everyone wrote the story of their life (which is what curriculum vitae means) in date order, starting with primary (or maybe secondary) school.

Now there are numerous ways of presenting them – and whole books devoted to the subject of the perfect CV. You could opt for chronological, reverse chronological, skills-based or professional models, among others. However, as a school or college leaver you won't have very much to include, so professional at least is out. Best to keep it simple. Here are two suggested formats.

## Chronological CV

**CURRICULUM VITAE**

| | |
|---|---|
| **NAME** | Joe Bloggs |
| **ADDRESS** | 10 Hall Drive, Anytown, Blankshire AN2 3YZ |
| **TELEPHONE** | 01728 135567 |
| **DATE OF BIRTH** | 5 June 1989 |
| **NATIONALITY** | British |

**EDUCATION**

| | |
|---|---|
| 2005-2007 | Anytown Sixth-Form College |
| 2007 | A levels in mathematics, sociology, history (to be taken in June) |
| 2006 | AS levels French (D), mathematics (B), sociology (C), history (B) |
| 2000-2005 | John Martin Community School, Anytown |
| 2005 GCSE: | English language (C), French (C), mathematics (A), art (B), history (A), music (D), double science (B, B), geography (A) |

**SPARE-TIME ACTIVITIES**

Captain of college football team; member of college orchestra; member of the outdoor pursuits group.

**EMPLOYMENT EXPERIENCE**

June 2004 Work experience, organised by school, at the Anytown Leisure Centre.

2005 – present. Weekend employment: Whitestones Bookshop instore coffee shop.

**SKILLS**

**IT** – CLAIT (Computer Literacy and Information Technology) diploma.

**Driving** – I am learning to drive and hold a provisional licence.

**Languages** – spoken German, enhanced by several visits to my pen-friend in Bavaria.

**INTERESTS**

**Amateur dramatics** – I belong to the Anytown Players. I have worked backstage and appeared in two plays.

**Sport** – I play regularly for the Olympics badminton club.

**Youth club** – As an active member of St Peter's Youth Club I am involved in community service and in charity fund-raising.

**REFEREES**

Mrs J Firth, Principal, Anytown Sixth-Form College, London Road, Anytown AN23 6AB.

Mr W Shakespeare, Manager, Whitestones Bookshop, The Precinct, Anytown AN2 3DQ.

(N.B. Never give anyone as a referee before obtaining their permission. Employers expect to see a headteacher or college principal as one of the referees.)

## Skills CV

**CURRICULUM VITAE**
**NAME**            Joe Bloggs
**ADDRESS**         10 Hall Drive, Anytown, Blankshire AN2 3YZ
**TELEPHONE**       01728 135567
**DATE OF BIRTH**   5 June 1989
**NATIONALITY**     British
**PERSONAL SKILLS AND CAPABILITIES**
              Good school attendance record
              Hard working
              Responsible and reliable
**OCCUPATONAL SKILLS**
              Computer literacy
              Customer service
              Work with children
**Information technology**
I have followed a CLAIT course (Computer Literacy and Information Technology).
**Customer service**
I have worked in a small coffee shop inside a book shop where I was responsible for welcoming customers, offering them newspapers to read and taking their orders.
**Work with children**
As part of my Community Sports Leader award scheme I have coached children between the ages of 8 and 13 in a number of sports.
**QUALIFICATIONS**
GCSEs 2005
              English language (C), French (C), mathematics (A), art (B), history (A), music (D), double science (B, B), geography (A)
AS levels 2006
              French (D), mathematics (B), sociology (C), history (B)
A levels to be taken, 2007 mathematics, sociology, history
**EDUCATION**
John Martin Community School Anytown, 2000-2005
Anytown Sixth-Form College, 2005-2007
**REFEREES**
Mrs J Firth, Principal, Anytown Sixth-Form College, London Road, Anytown AN23 6AB.
Mr W Shakespeare, Manager, Whitestones Bookshop, The Precinct, Anytown AN2 3DQ.

## Tips

- Keep the style simple. Fancy fonts and the inclusion of drawings or diagrams can irritate. Use a standard, simple font like Arial or Times New Roman.

- Use good-quality paper.

- Use an 11- or 12-point font size.

- Keep it brief. One side of A4 if you can. Two at most.

- Justify the text – i.e. have both margins straight.

- Leave space between sections.

- Number the pages.

- Use separate sheets of paper. No writing on the reverse with a 'PTO' message.

- Check for spelling errors and typos.

You can find advice on preparing a CV at any of these websites:

- www.connexions-direct.com

- www.careersserviceni.com

- www.careers-scotland.org.uk

- www.careerswales.com

- www.monster.co.uk

- www.springboard.hobsons.co.uk

and probably on the website of your own Connexions/careers service.

# Application forms

Whether you are completing a formal application form, or sending a CV with a covering letter, you must remember that in most cases your application will be one of many on the human resources officer's desk. Don't run the risk of it being discarded without a fair chance because of a simple careless slip in presentation. Illegible writing, or the form arriving late, may sound trivial reasons for rejecting someone for a job, but if you can imagine yourself in a recruiter's position, having to whittle down a large pile of application forms to manageable proportions, you might be tempted to do the same. Equally important is to answer all the questions correctly and without mistakes if applying via the internet.

## Tips

- Do a first draft on a photocopy or offline. Mistakes can then be corrected before you tackle the real thing.

- Don't leave questions unanswered. If something doesn't apply, put 'Not applicable'. This proves that you have seen the question – and not simply ignored it.

Before you start filling in a formal application for a job that has been advertised, you should look carefully at the job description. The aim in filling in an application form is to be one of the people selected for interview, so it is worth taking a bit of trouble to maximise your chances.

Try to present yourself in a good light by making it clear that you know something about the company and what it does, and that you are aware of the requirements of the job. You should attempt to relate your interests, aptitudes and experience to these requirements and sound keen to get the job. Don't try to be clever or amusing. This is rarely the best way to draw attention to your application.

## Check it over carefully

Employers at the receiving end of applications often complain about their poor standard. So, taking time and trouble at this stage could well give you a head start over rivals with better academic qualifications.

It is worthwhile asking someone who knows you reasonably well to look at your application form before you send it off, to make sure you have presented yourself in the best possible way. They may even help you to correct the odd spelling mistake! It is easy to get too close to a task like this and develop blind spots. N.B. Don't rely on your computer's spell checker. If it is the American English version it will give you the American version of certain words like centre or licence.

If your job applications do not lead to interview offers, have a word with your personal/careers adviser and ask whether your technique could be brushed up.

# Interviews

If you have been successful at your first hurdle, now is your chance to have a closer look at the employer and the company, while they also have a close look at you. An interview is a two-way process. To repeat – the employer is looking at you, and you are looking at the company. You might decide that you don't want the job after you have found out more. This does happen.

To make the best of this opportunity, you will need to make careful preparations. Try to anticipate the questions the interviewer will ask and be prepared with your answers. Have some questions of your own ready as well. There are whole books written on the dos and don'ts of interviews: some of them may be in your school or college Connexions resource centre/careers library. But, here is a brief list.

## DOs and DON'Ts

**Do:**

- keep a copy of your application form so that you can remind yourself of what you wrote on it

- take a copy of your CV and Progress File with you

- find out all you can about the employer, the size of the company, its products, services, other branches and so on

- find out exactly where you are going, and arrive on time. If something beyond your control prevents this, telephone and explain

- dress sensibly, in keeping with the job you are applying for. Jeans and a sweatshirt do not go down well with bank managers! Would-be graphic designers need not wear pin-striped suits

- try to memorise the name of your interviewer and use it from time to time

- answer the question that is asked and do not volunteer irrelevant information

- speak clearly and confidently

- be prepared to talk about yourself and your interests. This may not always seem to be related to the job but the interviewer is trying to assess the kind of person you are, how you will react to responsibility, and how you will fit into the organisation.

**Don't:**

- sit down until you have been asked to do so

- fidget

- try to answer questions too quickly; take time to think

- answer just 'Yes' or 'No' to questions. Short answers make it hard work for the interviewer

- try to be too clever

- talk endlessly, so that the interviewer can't get a word in edgeways

- criticise your school or college – 'I didn't get the best grades because I had poor teaching' doesn't help. As far as the employer knows it is simply an excuse. (But 'We had three changes of physics teacher in two years' could possibly be slipped in.)

- pretend you know about something when you don't. It could be very embarrassing for you when questions become more detailed

- pretend to understand what the interviewer is saying if you don't; ask to have it repeated

- ask questions when you know the answer. For example, don't ask for information that is contained in the job description given to you by the employer

- be afraid to ask questions about prospects and training. Questions such as these show you are keen to get the job.

## What sorts of questions will you be asked?

Interviews vary, and it would be impossible to predict exactly what you will be asked. Some of the things you should be prepared to talk about are:

- where you live or have lived

- your education and your school

- your interests and hobbies

- school subjects – your likes and dislikes, your strengths and weaknesses

- exams and results

- your personality: how you get on with people of your own age, and with people of all ages and backgrounds

- your career choices and ambitions
- why you have applied to this particular company or organisation
- why you want this particular job
- any part-time work mentioned on your application form
- your mobility – in other words whether you would be prepared to move to other parts of the country for promotion.

## What should you ask your interviewer?

What you ask is as important as what you are asked. Your questions show your keenness to tackle the job. The answers will help you decide whether you want to take the job or not.

Here are some of the things you might want to ask about.

- More details of what the job involves. Which office or department would you work in? With whom would you be working? The name and position of your immediate boss.
- How the job might change over the next year or two?
- What training would there be for the job inside or outside the company?
- Are there any minimum qualifications? Will the job be dependent on your exam results?
- Who pays for training courses and other expenses involved?
- What are the future prospects?
- What will be your working hours and holidays? (If this is not clear in the job description.)
- What will your starting salary be and how will you be paid?
- What are the company benefits: are there pension schemes, sports facilities, etc?
- Can you see the place of work?
- When will you hear the result of the interview?

Tips

- If there is more than one person conducting the interview

– which is quite common – speak for most of the time to the person who asked you the question, but look at the others briefly too – to include them in your reply.

- At the end, thank the interviewer for seeing you.

# Competency-based applications and interviews

## What are they?

Procedures that are used by a lot of large companies and public-sector organisations. You could well come across them.

Basically, in competency-based recruitment and selection, candidates are given a list of competencies for a particular job and have to give examples of how they have performed each one. You may think that it is unrealistic to expect people straight from school or college to be able to do this, but students leaving higher-education courses are often expected to do so – and large organisations often use the same technique when selecting level 3 applicants.

Interview competency-based questions are usually looking for evidence of skills that need to be used in the job and often start with **'Describe a situation** where you had to...' or **'Give an example** of a situation in which you...'

Examples include:

- How do you organise your time and assess your priorities?
- Describe a difficult situation and what you did about it.
- How well do you work in a team?
- As a member of team, what role do you play?
- Give an example of how you have influenced a group.
- How do you respond to stress? Can you provide a recent example?
- How do you/would you get the best out of people?

You *can* demonstrate competencies – by drawing on experiences in part-time jobs, work experience, voluntary work and social activities. (In fact your friends who are applying to university are probably having to think of similar ideas to write on their UCAS forms to impress admissions tutors!)

Competencies are often checked out in other parts of the selection process –when candidates are often placed in small groups and asked to carry out certain tasks. They may be designed to assess leadership potential, ability to work in a team, creativity, ability to persuade and influence, etc.

If you turn to page 93 you can read about Melanie Helps' competency-based application form and the examples she used in her answers, while on page 230 you can see the examples Alex Hargreaves used to answer questions during his interview. Several other people who feature in this book describe some of the tasks they had to complete during selection days. Have a look at the career profiles of Kirk Armitt (page 173), Sarah Goodridge (page 192), Gemma Lawson (page 213), Eddy Tumath (page 225) and Gemma Wright (page 178). It does not matter if the career they are in does not particularly interest you. It is the selection process that is important.

# Chapter five

## Training and qualifications

## Training

The training you receive will vary from employer to employer. Large companies usually have training officers who make sure that employees receive relevant training and are encouraged to take appropriate examinations. You might find a planned training programme mapped out for you in such a company, with day release to college included.

The training offered by smaller employers is variable. Some train you very quickly. Some encourage you to study for examinations; others do not think them relevant.

However, if you choose an Advanced Apprenticeship programme you will find that whatever the size of the company you follow a planned programme, with assessments to be carried out, and that you work towards NVQs or SVQs. This is because small companies under the scheme are able to draw on the expertise of external training organisations. As an Apprentice you would also have to complete training logs and diaries, and produce a portfolio of evidence demonstrating that you have become competent in specified tasks. Louise Matson (page 128) and Alex Hargreaves (page 230), who are both following Advanced Apprenticeship programmes, describe their training.

On an Apprenticeship programme you would gain:

- an appropriate National Vocational Qualification

- key skills qualifications, e.g. working in teams, problem solving, communication and using new technology

- a technical certificate, usually validated by an organisation like BTEC or City and Guilds

- other qualifications specified by the particular occupation.

Do find out about training when you have your job interview. Once you've started work, if you begin to feel the training is inadequate, talk to your manager. Try to be actively involved in mapping out a career action plan. In some cases you may have to try to create your own training. (See the section 'Doing the best for yourself' later in this chapter.)

# Large companies

If you join a large company with a formal training scheme, you will probably have a planned programme lasting from one to two years. You will be looked after by both a training officer and individual managers in whose departments you work, and you will start with an induction course when you will be told all about the company, its products and services, and how it is organised. You will also be told about pay, pensions and company facilities, such as catering, sports, clubs, banking arrangements, etc. You may be shown around the premises. Advanced Apprentice Alex Hargreaves mentions this kind of induction process on page 230.

After induction training (which could last from half a day to a week) you are likely to be assigned to a particular department of the company. Within that department, one person will probably be responsible for your training. He or she will show you the ropes and tell you what is expected of you. You may stay in this department for two or three months. Throughout this period you may have regular training for a day or several half-days a week with the other newcomers. These training days could be in the company's training centre and organised by the training officer. They may cover some of the topics on the induction course in more detail, as well as other aspects of the company's procedures and practices.

*Examples of people featured in this book who trained or are training with large organisations include Kirk Armitt (page 173), Jake Harris (page 117), Alex Hargreaves (page 230), Samantha Hubbard (page 183), Sarah Goodridge (page 192), Louise Matson (page 128) and Gemma Wright (page 178).*

## Short courses

Your employer may send you on specific short courses. These could be opportunities for you to learn particular ways of doing things that are relevant to your job. For example, if you are working for a travel agent, you could be sent on a course run by an airline on ticketing procedures. If you are working in a store that is part of a large retail chain you could be sent on a company course to learn about accounts. In addition, some companies send their trainees on courses designed to encourage personal development. These could be courses such as the Outward Bound scheme, including hill walking, climbing, canoeing and other outdoor activities, or courses in particular skills such as public speaking.

## Finding out by doing

After you have completed a couple of months in one department or branch of an organisation, you could be moved to another one to learn about a different aspect of work. Throughout a one- or two-year training programme, you could be moved several times. During your training, you will be in constant contact with the training officer (or a mentor) who will make a regular review of your progress, usually in conjunction with the head of the section in which you have been working. Towards the end of your training period, the training officer will discuss with you where your strengths and interests lie, and what possibilities there are of a permanent job in a particular department. When you come to the end of your training, you should be able to move directly into your first responsible post.

*For examples of this kind of training, see the profiles of Kirk Armitt (page 173) who works for the Arcadia Group, Alex Hargreaves (page 230) who works for Bentley Motors and Jake Harris (page 117) who is with McDonald's.*

# Smaller companies

The training outlined above is typical of a large company or organisation that has a formal training scheme. If you join a smaller company, it could well be very different. However, you should find that someone will give you a short induction or briefing about what the company does and other details. You will then be assigned to a department and a particular member of staff and left under his or her supervision. You should still have discussions and/or appraisals with the training or personnel officer, or with the manager. If there is no formal training scheme, you can make a big difference to your own training by showing keenness to learn and by asking how different departments work. If you ask questions such as these, it is likely that they will allow you to visit other departments in the company to see what goes on. This is how Sally Parker (page 150) trained.

You may or may not be offered day release by the company. Where possible, you should try to ask for day-release training as it gives you a chance to improve your qualifications. If you are in a field of work where there is a recognised qualification, you may be at a disadvantage later on if you haven't obtained it. Some smaller companies are obviously reluctant to lose an employee for one day or half a day a week. They can also find it expensive, particularly as you will be over 18 and the company will therefore have to pay fees at the local college – unless they take you on under the Apprenticeship scheme, in which case they will receive some assistance. You may find the employer would be more amenable if you offered to pay some of your fees, or if you paid the fees and they promised to reimburse you later, when you had passed the exams. Other employers may want you to work for at least a year before starting a day-release scheme. In the career profiles, you will read about a wide variety of arrangements that people have made with employers.

*People who are on day release include Tom Lengthorn (page 186), Matthew Morfoot (page 206), Greg Rogers (page 189) and Jake Wilks (page 209).*

# Doing the best for yourself

Don't panic if you are not placed on a formal training scheme. There are plenty of successful people whose first career step was simply to get a foot in the door – who were willing to start at the bottom in an organisation they wanted to work for. Your own first job might seem limited in scope, but it is a starting point and it could well lead on to a range of other things.

If you do start 'at the bottom', there are several ways to progress. It may be that the company has a planned training scheme that you can apply for internally, once you have shown what you can do in the job. If, though, the company doesn't seem to have any plans for your progress, then you must take the initiative for your own career development.

You can:

- keep an eye on opportunities to widen your experience

- learn as many new skills as you can

- offer to take some responsibility

- look out for prospects for promotion.

If none of these does the trick and you begin to think that you are in a dead-end job, you should consider moving to another company. The work experience you have had will probably be useful in other organisations, and the knowledge you gain both about yourself and the working world will make seeking a second job a lot easier. But remember that you are dependent on your first employer for references, so don't deliberately antagonise anybody! It would be a good idea to talk over any plans or hopes for a career move or job change with an adviser at your Connexions/careers centre.

One of the interesting things about careers is that people have such a wide variety of experiences – as you will see from the career profiles. But whatever situation you find yourself in, it is very much up to you to make the best of it for yourself. Some of the people described in this book, who were on formally-organised training schemes, found that when they were assigned to individual departments they were in part regarded as responsible for their own learning and had to discuss their targets with their line managers – and then set about achieving them.

# Examinations and qualifications

It's very important to realise that if you take a job that includes good training – and this is what you should be aiming for, in order not to waste your qualifications – you may find that you have not said goodbye to exams. (Choosing not to go to university full time does not necessarily mean that you won't be participating in higher education! You have simply chosen a different route – and in fact around 40% of all students in higher education now study part time.) Many employers will expect you to study for further qualifications, often in your own time. In some careers, training and qualifications are prescribed by a professional body, such as the Royal Town Planning Institute or the accountancy bodies. They specify the length of training and type of experience you must receive, and set exams that must be passed if you wish to become fully qualified.

## Examinations

In certain careers it is essential to pass exams in order to become fully qualified and practise a profession, the major ones being:

- accountancy (although there are good opportunities for 'part qualified' accountants)
- air traffic control
- dispensing opticians
- engineering
- Merchant Navy
- surveying
- town and country planning.

In other professions passing the examinations is not compulsory in itself, but almost invariably essential for promotion (banking and insurance are two examples).

Not every career involves examinations. Sometimes there are no particularly appropriate ones; sometimes individual employers are free to decide whether or not to encourage trainees to take them.

In retailing, for example, there are no compulsory or specialist exams, although some employers would prefer you to take a business studies certificate. In computing, advertising and marketing, qualifications are available and may be useful for promotion or when changing jobs. In some career areas there are no relevant exams organised by professional bodies, but you might be encouraged to work towards a more general qualification such as a BTEC/SQA Higher National Certificate or Diploma in business. Study is done through day or block release, or by evening classes, or through distance learning.

## Some definitions

### Apprenticeships

Apprenticeships are offered on a salaried basis, or for certain programmes, such as the Foundation Modern Apprenticeship in Wales and some preparatory programmes, on a training-allowance basis. (That is – most people are recruited as employees and trained through the Apprenticeship programme; others receive a training allowance from the government.) Trainees learn their particular jobs, together with general vocational skills that can be applied to any job, such as problem solving and teamwork. They may also learn special skills such as foreign languages.

Alex Hargreaves (page 230) is doing one in logistics; Louise Matson (page 128) is following one in hotel management. Lee Irwin (page 196) is training this way with British Telecom. If you have level 3 qualifications you should be aiming for the level known as Advanced Apprenticeship. (In Wales, similar programmes are called Foundation Modern Apprenticeships and Modern Apprenticeships, and in Scotland you should enquire about Modern Apprenticeships and the Skillseekers' Initiative.)

Some people are recruited directly onto Apprenticeship programmes; others may start them later. Louise Matson for example had already completed her employer's own training programme when her company suggested that she should do further training through an Advanced Apprenticeship.

### Day release

One day (usually stretching into the evening) each week is spent at a college of further education or technology for tuition leading to professional or vocational exams. Courses usually last for two or three years and lead to qualifications awarded by validating bodies such as Edexcel (BTEC qualifications) and SQA, or professional bodies such as the Association of Accounting Technicians or the Chartered Institute of Management Accountants. Lynn Elliott (page 97) qualified through this route in accountancy and Matthew Morfoot (page 206) is studying for a degree by attending university one day each week.

### Block release

This is very similar to day release, but trainees attend college for longer periods of several weeks at a time. Shipping companies are examples of employers that use this method.

## Distance learning

If there is no suitable course, or if your employer will not give day release, you could consider taking a distance-learning course. This includes other methods of teaching such as videos and online tuition. It may be supplemented by short residential tutorial courses. The Association of British Correspondence Colleges can supply a list of relevant courses and colleges. Distance-learning courses are hard work and require a lot of self-motivation.

More people give up on this route than on any other, but many also qualify this way each year. Sarah Goodridge (page 192) is an example of a success story.

## And some qualifications

**Higher National Diplomas** (HNDs) are roughly equivalent to the first two years of a Bachelor's degree programme. Some are held in colleges of further or higher education, but most are run by universities that were once polytechnics and that designed courses relevant to local employers. There are currently over 80 HNDs, across 21 work-related sectors. Business, engineering, computing and IT are the subjects currently in greatest demand.

Many HNDs are being modified and converted into foundation degrees (see below).

**Higher National Certificate (HNC)** programmes are at the same standard as HNDs, but cover less ground since they contain fewer modules. People at work often choose to take an HNC – and study the modules that are appropriate to their job.

**Foundation degree** programmes are available in over 1600 work-related subjects and a further 800 are planned. They have been developed by the higher education sector with employers, and give you the skills needed at associate-professional and higher-technician level. Those in employment can study through part-time or distance learning.

If you do an HNC, HND or foundation degree you will have the option of converting to a degree by further study, usually by starting the second or third year of a related degree course. Some foundation degrees have already replaced HND courses, but in some areas both qualifications exist side by side.

You may or may not have a choice as to whether you do a Higher National qualification or a foundation degree. Employers frequently have their own preferences – for qualification and for subject.

## Part-time study is hard work

Many of the people featured in the career profiles made the point that studying for professional qualifications was hard work. The time you would need to put in shouldn't be underestimated.

Most people find that they need to put in the equivalent of one day each week to keep on top of assignments and revision. Many often find it difficult to start studying after a day at work, but gradually begin to work out their own approach. Some people find that setting aside regular evenings works best for them. Others prefer to work at weekends. The less well organised work frantically before a project or essay is due or as an exam approaches.

Whatever method you choose, the key is to work out a way that suits you – and learn as soon as possible to achieve the right balance between work and social life.

To sum up – training this way is not a soft option. If you decide on it, you will probably be working harder than your friends at university!

# From student to earner

Many people have found the start of their working lives rather boring. A job can be very different from school or college where the timetable was varied. In addition, after the kind of supervision you have been used to at school, and the level of academic work you have been tackling, you could find the first few months in a job quite a change.

If this happens to you don't lose heart. Most people find the transition to work hard, whether they leave school with no qualifications or whether they are graduates in their first job! No matter how much careers education you have had and how carefully you have prepared yourself for going to work, you can only learn to cope with awkward customers or stubborn supervisors by actually doing a job.

Good luck!

# Further information

**Association of British Correspondence Colleges** – PO Box 17926, London SW19 3WB. Tel: 020 8544 9559. www.homestudy.org.uk

**Edexcel Foundation (BTEC)** – One90 High Holborn, London WC1V 7BH. Tel: 0870 240 9800. www.edexcel.org.uk

**Scottish Qualifications Authority** – Hanover House, The Optima Building, 58 Robertson Street, Glasgow G2 8DQ. Tel: 0845 279 1000. www.sqa.org.uk

## Reading

Consult up-to-date resources, such as those listed below and in Chapter seven, to find out which qualifications relate to particular careers:

*Careers 2007* – published by Trotman

*The Penguin Careers Guide*

and, for information on the availability of courses use databases or directories of local courses, or national databases such as www.learndirect.co.uk or the Course Discover database. These may be available in schools or colleges or in Connexions/careers centres.

# Chapter six

## Enterprise. Working for yourself

Some people dream of running their own businesses. They value their independence. They want to be their own boss. They may see themselves building up a company and employing other people – or they may simply want to work alone or with a partner.

## Do you see yourself as an entrepreneur?

If so, have you got what it takes?

Nobody would pretend that it is easy to go it alone – especially when you are straight from school or college and have neither training, experience nor capital. It's in no way an easy option. First, self-starters need to have an idea. Then they need the know-how to make it work, plus the determination and courage to carry on when things look bleak. They have to think out a business from scratch and make it work; cope with advertising and marketing; balance the financial books; and cope with problems.

In fact, most people who start up in business on their own gain their first business experiences in another job (making their mistakes and learning from them at someone else's expense!). Then they adapt a particular skill or special knowledge to a new idea, or they branch out on their own in the same line of business as the company they had been working for. Both Roger Chunnoo and Stuart Ebdy, who you can read about in Chapter sixteen, did exactly that.

Others have used the knowledge they gained on a college course or during a period of work experience on a government training scheme. On the other hand, there are young people who start up on their own, without previous experience.

Generally speaking, it will probably be easier to think of a business idea if you have relevant applied or vocational qualifications at level 3 rather than academic ones. Art and design, photography, business or sports qualifications all lend themselves more readily to providing a marketable service than do academic qualifications. But you could always make use of an interest, hobby or qualifications (for example in sports coaching, cookery, beauty) that you have obtained outside your level 3 course. Or – you could obtain a vocational qualification while employed in another job.

What sort of business could you run? That is up to you. However, the simplest ideas can often be the best and will not require much initial outlay. How about:

- inventing computer games
- offering garden design services
- being a mobile beauty therapist
- becoming a personal fitness trainer
- offering tuition in computing to nervous beginners? (Yes. There are plenty – mainly in the generation above you!)

These are just a few ideas that have the advantage of not needing too much initial equipment. An added benefit is that you would carry them out either at clients' premises or from your own bedroom (provided that you have your parents' support, that is).

## Points to consider

To run your own business, you need to deal with a variety of considerations, such as your product or service, your market, premises, equipment, cash accounts, tax, loans, etc.

You will need to ask yourself some basic questions.

- What product or service can I sell?
- To which customers?
- How do I find them?
- How do I advertise?
- Who would I be in competition with?
- Where will I be based? (Can you work from home initially?)
- How do I find out about keeping financial records?
- Where can I raise some money to help me start up?
- How do I survive financially until I start to show a profit?

### The harsh facts

Twenty per cent of new businesses fail to make it to their sixth anniversary. The majority of those that fail do so in the first year of trading. Most of those that collapse do so due to a lack of proper financial advice.

SO, YOU ARE LIKELY TO NEED HELP. It is important to seek as much advice as you can before launching out on your own.

Fortunately, there are government schemes to help people become self-employed and many agencies to help with advice (e.g. Business Link).

You could try to set up on your own, in partnership with others, or through a cooperative venture. For details of help available ask at your local Jobcentre Plus, library or Citizens Advice Bureau.

In addition, there are many books on setting up your own business that might be a starting point to help you consider what is likely to be involved. Your local library should have a number of books on the subject.

## Two important sources of help

Especially relevant to you are two organisations that are dedicated to assisting young people in business start-up.

### The Prince's Trust

The Prince's Trust is a charity that awards grants and low-interest loans to people between the ages of 18-30 who are either unemployed or working for less than 16 hours a week. They must be able to produce a realistic business plan and convince Trust officials of their commitment. It is a 'last resort' funding organisation. In order to be eligible for assistance you would have to prove that you had tried all other possible sources (for example, banks and your own family).

You must also have attended a short business course (the Trust's local office, a Jobcentre Plus or Connexions/careers centre could give you information on this) and have prepared a business plan (see next page). The maximum amount of loan to any one business is £5,000 to a partnership or £4,000 to a sole trader. Test marketing grants (non-repayable) of £250 are offered, and in special circumstances there may be further grants of up to £1,500 per business.

In addition to financial assistance you would also receive practical advice from local business people who give their time voluntarily to the Trust and act as mentors. Last year the Trust helped 12,793 young people to start their own businesses.

N.B. In Scotland, business start-up support is through the Prince's Scottish Youth Business Trust for 18-25 year olds.

### Shell LiveWIRE

Shell LiveWIRE is a national scheme that encourages people aged 16-30 to become entrepreneurs. It was begun by Shell UK Limited in 1982 and since then has assisted over 600,000 young people to start their own businesses, by providing free local advice, information and business support for their ideas. At the heart of Shell LiveWIRE is a support network that delivers insight and advice. It offers both tailored and general support and helps young people to develop useful relationships with others like them – who understand the challenges faced by new businesses and young entrepreneurs.

Among successful 'Shell LiveWIREs' are bungee-jumping organisers, caterers, recruitment agencies, restaurant owners, software producers, stockbrokers, funeral directors and makers of luxury chocolates.

If you contact Shell LiveWIRE you will receive:

- a free business information start-up pack

- free advice from a local business adviser (they have 82 local coordinators who organise one-to-one advice)

- access to information and articles on the internet

- sums of money – if you are lucky enough to win one of their regional or national competitions.

Sixty-five per cent of 'Shell LiveWIREs' are still trading after four years.

Fraser Edgar of Shell LiveWIRE says 'Shell LiveWIRE's mission is to help unearth and support the young entrepreneurs of today who will create the jobs, wealth and innovations of tomorrow. We do this through marrying peer-to-peer inspiration and encouragement with practical nuts-and-bolts help that can only come from business people who understand the challenges of building a business.'

You can read about some of the success stories on the Shell LiveWIRE website (www.shell-livewire.org).

# Your business plan

Whichever source you approach with a request for a loan or other type of funding, the chances are that you will be asked for your business plan? What is this?

Simply – a document outlining your plans and start-up proposals. It will show that you have thought matters through and are aware of the steps you will have to take. On it should be outlined:

- a description of your product or service

- a list of your anticipated start-up costs (to cover rent, equipment, tools, stationery, publicity, etc)

- your marketing plan – have you researched the need for your product? Who will buy it? What is the local competition? How will you price it and on what basis? (list costs of materials and labour)

- a list of your expected living expenses during the start-up period

- a cash-flow forecast (money expected to come in and money needed to pay bills)

- a trading-profit forecast
- business-development plans
- and your personal history – your age, experience, training and qualifications.

The plan has to look professional – so you should seek help and advice in preparing it.

# Further information

Your local branch of the Learning and Skills Council (England), National Council for Education and Training in Wales (ELWa – Education Learning Wales) or LEC (Local Enterprise Companies – Scotland).

## The Prince's Trust

**The Prince's Trust** – 18 Park Square East, London NW1 4LH. Tel: 020 7543 1234. www.princes-trust.org.uk

**The Prince's Trust Cymru** – Baltic House, Mount Stuart Square, Cardiff CF10 5FH. Tel: 029 2043 7000. www.princes-trust.org.uk

**The Prince's Trust Northern Ireland** – Block 5, Jennymount Court, North Derby Street, Belfast BT15 3HN. Tel: 028 9074 5454. www.princes-trust.org.uk

**The Prince's Trust Scotland** – 1st Floor, The Guildhall, 57 Queen Street, Glasgow G1 3EN. Tel: 0141 204 4409. www.psybt.org.uk

OR you can call the freephone number 0800 842 842 to be put in touch with The Prince's Trust office in your area.

## Shell LiveWIRE

**Shell LiveWIRE England** – Unit 15 Design Works, William Street, Felling, Gateshead NE10 0J. Tel: 0191 423 6229. www.shell-livewire.org

**Shell LiveWIRE Ireland** – 5 Airport Road, Belfast BT3 9EU. Tel: 028 9055 3802. www.shell-livewire.org

**Shell LiveWIRE Scotland** – 6a Queens Road, Aberdeen AB15 4Z. Tel: 01224 626373. www.shell-livewire.org

OR you can call 08457 573 252 (local call rate).

# Chapter seven

## How to find out more

More information can be obtained from your personal/careers adviser or careers teacher and from the publications listed below, which should be available in your school or college, your Connexions/careers centre, local careers office or public library.

You can also get more information from the addresses given in the career notes at the end of each career profile. For careers not covered by a profile, you can obtain information from the relevant professional body or from your nearest Connexions/careers centre.

# Reading: careers reference books

- *Careers 2007* – Trotman Publishing, revised annually.
- The Penguin Careers Guide

These are careers directories, describing job content, entry qualifications and training methods in all major career areas.

- *Working In* series – published by Connexions; new editions published by VT Lifeskills. These books describe jobs in the career area of each title and include up to 15 career profiles.

- *Job Book* – Hobsons Publishing. This contains information on, and advertisements from, employers who are recruiting, as well as advice on job hunting and making applications.

# Information on computer

- JED (Job Explorer database)
- KeyCLIPS
- KUDOS
- Odyssey Plus

These systems may be available in your school or college.

# Useful websites

- www.connexions-direct.com
- www.careersserviceni.com (Northern Ireland)
- www.careers-scotland.org.uk (Scotland)
- www.careerswales.com (Wales)
- www.monster.co.uk
- www.springboard.hobsons.co.uk

and the website of your Connexions/careers centre.

# Index of career profiles

All the subjects of these profiles left school or college after following an advanced-level course. They are generally between 19 and 25 years of age, although a few are around 30. Some had good enough qualifications to go to university but chose to start their careers without a degree. Some planned their career applications in the second year of their course; others applied for higher education and changed their minds or failed to get the grades required for the course they wanted. A few started on courses in higher education and one or two were unemployed for some time before getting a job.

The profiles cover a wide variety of people in a wide variety of jobs. They are in ones that you might be interested in considering. None of the people could be described as 'typical'. They are all individuals. They all had their own reasons for their job choice; they were all in different individual circumstances. They have their own very personal reactions to their jobs and their working environments.

If you are interested in their jobs, the notes at the end of each section should give you some idea of how to find out more about them and about other closely-related careers. It was not possible to cover all possible opportunities in the profiles, but the reading list at the end of each profile will give you some sources to look at for other ideas. Everyone seemed to enjoy talking about their jobs. Most people do. Sometimes it's hard to stop them! Don't be afraid to track down people in your area who are doing the type of job that interests you. They would probably be only too happy to help.

## Career profile chapters

### Chapter eight: Business management and public administration
Fiona King page 91
Human resources administrator – Neal's Yard Remedies Ltd

Melanie Helps page 93
Business planning support officer – MOD

Lynn Elliott page 97
Financial project consultant – County Treasurer's Department,
Hampshire County Council

Emma Turner page 100
Manager, accounts reconciliation team – HM Revenue and Customs

Anna Bantin page 103
Administrative assistant (currently working in recruitment) – Foreign
and Commonwealth Office

Linda Brockwell page 107
Housing officer – Martlet Homes

Tamarin Gibbs page 111
Personal adviser – Connexions Wiltshire and Swindon

## Chapter nine: Creative and leisure services

Rob Wilson page 115
Photographer – Jonathan Fisher Photography

Jake Harris page 117
Operations consultant, McDonald's Restaurants

Lindsay Currie page 121
Library assistant – Shepherd and Wedderburn

Sam Myers page 125
Advertising TV production assistant – Saatchi & Saatchi

Louise Matson page 128
Trainee assistant manager – Shearings Hotels

Craig Cotterill page 132
Corporate events manager – Alton Towers Park

## Chapter ten: Finance and insurance

Will McAlpine page 135
Acting branch manager – Skipton Building Society

Darren Fagan page 139
Senior business manager – NatWest

Fiona Catling page 144
Semi-senior accounting technician – Hayles, Farrar & Partners

## Chapter eleven: The Services, security and law

## Chapter twelve: Retailing, marketing and sales

## Chapter thirteen: Scientific and technical

## Chapter fourteen: Construction, surveying and property

## Chapter fifteen: Transport, travel and logistics

## Chapter sixteen: Working for yourself

# Chapter eight

# Business management and public administration

## Fiona King
### Human resources administrator – Neal's Yard Remedies Ltd

While studying for an AVCE in business studies (now applied business A level) Fiona became interested in human resources (HR). Fiona has always enjoyed helping other people, and decided not to go to university because of the cost, so a role within HR seemed perfect for her.

### First job

After completing her AVCE Fiona began working as an administrative assistant and started studying for her Certificate in Personnel Practice (CPP) on a part-time basis. 'The CPP gives you a basic understanding of the HR function and employment law.'

Human resources was the area of business she found the most interesting. Fiona also had the opportunity to shadow the HR officer where she worked, and this gave her a greater understanding of the work involved in HR.

### Next stage

'I was approached by an employment agency who saw my CV on the internet and asked if they could put me forward for a job with Neal's Yard Remedies. I was offered a first-stage interview with the acting HR manager. After this I was offered a second interview, which involved completing a work-based task.' Fiona got the job and has been working as an HR administrator for eight months!

## Fiona's role

In the first week of her new job Fiona learned all about Neal's Yard Remedies, including their products and the ethos of the company. One of her first tasks was to learn and understand the weekly and monthly payroll system. 'My daily tasks include timesheets and payroll administration, absence monitoring, new employee administration, customer service and reporting HR statistical information. I am responsible for ensuring all HR administration is carried out in a timely and accurate manner. It is a busy and varied role, encompassing all aspects of HR. Service to our employees (about 280) and customers is of key importance. The great thing about my job is that every day is different. Because my role is so varied, I am gaining valuable generalist experience in a job that I love, which I believe is invaluable for my future career prospects.'

## Career development

'Since joining Neal's Yard Remedies, my experience has grown immensely. This is due to the wealth of experience of the people that I work with. I have also taken part in workshops; for example, the last workshop I attended covered how to use an effective personal development plan, and how to set meaningful and realistic objectives. Later this year, I hope to attend some external workshops on employment law to further my knowledge and understanding. Within the next year I want to progress on to an adviser/officer role with more responsibility, and I would like to develop my employment law experience. Within the next two to three years I would like to undertake a degree in HR management, while working, and gain full membership of the Chartered Institute of Personnel and Development (CIPD) so I can develop my career and experience further.'

## Advice

'For those interested in a career in HR, it is a very challenging yet rewarding role. I would advise that they should complete the Certificate in Personnel Practice (CPP) to gain the valuable basic understanding of the HR function and employment law. I would also advise that they become a member of the CIPD as this is so valued within the field of HR.'

## Career note

Human resources management, or personnel management as it was traditionally called, is about recruiting, training and managing an organisation's workforce. The work of the HR manager can vary. Human resources departments are responsible for many different areas, such as recruitment, training, employee relations and salary administration. A large firm may have separate HR staff for aspects such as training, recruitment and employee relations. In a small company, one person may carry out all these functions. It is also possible to work for a specialist HR consultancy, providing HR services to other companies.

It may be possible to work your way up by joining an HR department in a clerical or secretarial post – usually with good GCSEs, or A levels or equivalent – and studying part time. Good communication skills and a knowledge of employment law are important.

## Further information

**Chartered Institute of Personnel and Development** – 151 The Broadway, London SW19 1JQ. Tel: 020 8612 6200. www.cipd.co.uk/careers

The CIPD's fortnightly publication *People Management* is a good source of vacancy information and can be viewed online.

## Related careers

Management

Training

Jobs with trade unions

Working for an employment agency

# Melanie (Mel) Helps
## Business planning support officer – MOD

Mel left Clarendon School in Trowbridge with A levels in English, history and psychology. She had a place to read history at Bristol University but decided during her gap year that she no longer wanted it. She says 'University was heavily promoted at school. It was the only after-A level option that was discussed. If you were not interested in university then you were kind of forgotten. They did not discuss college courses or Apprenticeships. You were left to find out the options for yourself. I decided that I wanted to get some real job experience before committing to a university course. Also, I did not want to get into debt when I was unsure of what I wanted to do at the end of a degree course. What I did want, I decided, was an office job but one in which I would be helping others.'

So Mel joined the Civil Service where she has been for two-and-a-half years. It was her grandfather who saw the job advertisement in a local paper and told her about it. At the time Mel was working in a temporary job to finance a CLAIT course, which she felt would add to her CV. The Civil Service job was in the local office of the Pensions Service.

## Application

Mel had to complete a *competency-based* application form. 'There were four questions designed to assess whether I had the right qualities for the job – and they demanded full answers. One, for example, asked about evidence of teamworking skills, so I used the team-building part of the Duke of Edinburgh Award that I had done to answer that one. Another one asked about my skill in time management. I used my planning of my A level revision timetable for that one.' Mel was selected for interview at which she was asked questions that required her to expand on what she had written on the form. She had kept a photocopy and re-read it, working out possible answers the evening before the interview.

## First job

Mel joined as an administrative officer and learned how to process retirement pensions. 'Four months and four days before a person reaches state retirement age the Pensions Service contacts them and says that an application form is on its way to them. When the forms come back we have to check them and fill in any missing gaps or clear up any inconsistencies. I had to learn how to read National Insurance Contribution records and understand what they meant. I might have found, for example, that someone had a contributions gap. That might have been while they were receiving some kind of state benefit (in which case they should have been credited with contributions) or that there was a gap in contributions from an employer. Once the customer had been contacted to find out what they had been doing at that time, I would have to ring the employer or the relevant benefits agency and get the record amended. I would also have to explain the results of my investigation to the person claiming the pension. I did a lot of telephone work – and quite a lot of face-to-face meetings with people who came into the office. Most people were very nice, especially if I was helping to increase their pensions – but as in every job you meet some people who have complaints.' Mel learned the work on a 20-week training programme in the office and then moved on to a pensions section. She found that she needed assistance at first and often had to ask her line manager for advice. But her confidence increased with every phone call and she soon became competent.

## Career move

Mel felt that she needed to move to another department in order to progress, and put in a request to transfer to the Ministry of Defence (MOD). She was successful at interview when a vacancy arose, and for the last three months has been working for the MOD in her present job. In business support her duties are very varied. 'One of my principal duties is being responsible for health and safety in my team, which has about 80 people. I have to make sure that we are compliant with the Secretary of State's Health and Safety Policy Statement. This includes things like arranging display screen assessment tests for everyone, checking that no one is working in potentially dangerous conditions – with trailing wires, for instance, or cupboards that could fall over. Carrying out risk assessments for all the team can mean visiting different offices (in different towns). I'm also responsible for security, and making sure that anyone who takes anything out of the office – like a laptop for instance – has the proper authorisation. I also set up computer access and valid email accounts for all new people in the team and I help the finance manager with forecasts and staff costs.

When I come in in the morning I first check my emails to see if there is anything urgent about health or security to be dealt with. Then, depending on what there is, I can do all sorts of things for the rest of the day. No two days are ever the same. I might help the finance section on some days, especially at the end of the month. During the middle of the month, I may be ordering software for individuals to help with their work. I also help my line manager to organise any office or equipment moves. Sometimes I am asked to do something by my line manager and this normally takes priority, but otherwise I am free to organise my own work and decide in which order to do things.'

## Flexible hours

One of the bonuses of Mel's job is flexitime. She must start work between 7.30am and 10.00am and finish between 4pm and 6.30pm. She must also take a break of at least 30 minutes between 12.00 noon and 2pm.

Otherwise she is free to choose her hours – and normally works between 8am and 4pm. A huge bonus is that she is allowed to credit overtime and exchange it for days off. Last year she collected ten days in this way.

## What does Mel like about her job?

'I like working for an employer who is committed to developing my skills. The Civil Service works hard at being an equal opportunities employer. I also like working in a big organisation and getting to meet lots of people. I appreciate the fact that once you are in the Civil Service qualifications don't matter too much. Experience and ability can get you promotion.'

## The future

Mel intends to stay in the MOD and hopes to be promoted to a junior-management grade within the next two to three years – when she has sampled more jobs and decided where her interests lie. She has not ruled out university altogether, and may do a history degree. But it will be through the Open University.

## Career note

Students with 18+ qualifications can apply to join the Civil Service as trainee junior managers (known as executive officers in some departments). Entry is very competitive, however, and many join at the lower grade of administrative officer and work their way up through internal promotion as Mel is doing.

Administrative officers are recruited locally, so you should ask your Connexions/careers service for information or look in the local paper for advertisements. You can get general information from both the central Civil Service address given below and directly from individual departments.

## Further information

Because of the breadth of the Civil Service there is no central contact for information. You will find contacts for individual departments on the website www.careers.civil-service.gov.uk

## Related careers

Local government administration

National Health Service administration

# Lynn Elliott
## Financial project consultant – County Treasurer's Department, Hampshire County Council

Lynn, who did A levels at school in Wokingham, Berkshire, never intended to go to university. Instead, she researched management training schemes and began work with a large department-store group. This was not exactly what she had anticipated. 'I worked in several different departments – but found it totally unexciting. However, I had one A level pass (in history) and this enabled me to take a Higher National Certificate (HNC) in distribution on day release, sponsored by the company. I stayed for two years to get the qualification, then left.'

Lynn analysed her skills, and realised that she was numerate and had enjoyed the financial topics on the HNC course. She therefore decided to move into accountancy and found a job as a trainee accounting technician with a local council. Thanks to her HNC she was exempt from most of the exam papers and quickly qualified. She next applied for a job as a development accountant in the authority's corporate finance department, and to her surprise, got it. 'It was a senior position and they took a chance on me.' Lynn enjoyed the job, which included VAT work, pension fund and insurance accounting, plus financial projects within the department. She was also the corporate finance IT network supervisor. About 25% of her time was spent in treasury management. This, she explains, means managing the cash in an organisation. 'In a local authority this can involve handling very large sums. You have to implement a strategy for borrowing and lending to manage the peaks and troughs so that the authority always has sufficient money to pay its bills, which can be considerable – for example, at the end of the month when salaries are due – but does not have cash lying idle. Incoming sums can be large too, as on the date when all the district councils forward their council tax payments to county councils. Part of my job was to lend and borrow some of our surplus to make money from it (which local authorities are able to do within certain limits). I was constantly on the phone – and for one hour first thing – to London dealers, and managed sums of £20 million in total, with individual deals of up to £5 million each. The more usual day sum was £1-5million.'

## Qualifying

Lynn began studying for the Chartered Institute of Public Finance and Accountancy (CIPFA) qualification. In this she was assisted by her employer who gave her day release – but not, she says, by the college she attended in the first instance. 'It was not good. I struggled – and had to re-sit one paper. However, when a new head of department was appointed I was sent instead to CIPFA's own training centre in London. This was so much better. They give excellent tuition and are really geared up to getting people through exams'. Lynn now acts as a voluntary tutor for CIPFA, for a few days each year. 'I wanted to give something back, so I help students who are in their final year. They have to give a ten-minute presentation and answer questions for one hour on the 8,000 word project they have carried out. I sit on a panel that does a mock session where they can get the practice, build confidence and learn from their mistakes.'

Study for the exams was time consuming. Lynne estimates that she spent two evenings each week and most Sundays on college work. By the time it came to the final examination year most of her free time was spent in studying.

## Consultancy work

For the last three years Lynn has been in her present job in Winchester. As a consultant she works for different departments within the county council, or for other public-sector organisations such as the Hampshire Constabulary, Fire and Rescue Service, Harbour Board or Probation Service – and for several voluntary organisations. She usually has several projects to manage at any one time. How does this work? 'Departments can purchase blocks of consultancy time – a set number of days over the year. There are seven qualified accountants plus trainee accountants in the team, and the group manager allocates us to projects according to our availability and our particular skills. Of course, if a project comes up that I am keen to do and I have the time then I can bid for it.

I have to be a very good time manager as I can be juggling up to 12 different projects. I enjoy doing this and love the variety of working on very different topics at the same time. Examples of projects include one for the education department to determine the total cost of IT equipment throughout the department and in all the schools; another for social services, coordinating and managing a framework for establishing partnership arrangements with the health authority, voluntary organisations and charities; and making two funding bids for European transnational environmental projects on behalf of the authority. One involved a trip to Brussels. Every project involves an initial meeting with staff from the relevant department. I have to establish what they want to achieve, get all the necessary information – then work with them to complete the work within the required time frame.'

## Advice from Lynn

'Don't underestimate the time needed to spend on study for professional qualifications.

Don't assume that accountancy is all about playing with numbers! It can be, if that is what you want. That is one of the benefits of the qualification. You can use it to get the kind of job that is right for you. My present job involves strong communication skills. Working with so many different people means that I have to be able to establish relationships very quickly. I need to ask questions in the right way to get the information I need, and I have to be sure that I can explain things to people who are not financial experts.'

## Career note

People who hold the CIPFA professional qualification are known as chartered public finance accountants. In order to register as a CIPFA trainee you would need to have a minimum of three GCSEs/S grades at A\*-C/1-3 and two A levels/three H grades, including English and maths at either level. Alternative qualifications include BTEC/SQA national level awards and NVQs/SVQs at level 3.

The scope of local government has been reduced since national government policy has encouraged more services to move out of local council control. Schools are less dependent on the education authority, and refuse departments, parks and many other services are being put out to tender to private organisations. If you are thinking about local government as an employer, you ought also to think of the non-local government organisations now being asked to deliver public services.

However, there are still many local government careers for many different types of professional. The treasurer's department is just one. It is worth emphasising that, once you become a local government employee in one department, you will have access to early information about vacancies arising in other departments in your authority and will be able to apply for any for which you are qualified.

## Further information

**The Chartered Institute of Public Finance and Accountancy** - 3 Robert Street, London WC2N 6RL. Tel: 020 7543 5600. www.cipfa.org.uk

**Local Government Employers** - Local Government House, Smith Square, London SW1P 3HZ. Tel: 020 7187 7373. www.lg-employers.gov.uk

**Convention of Scottish Local Authorities (COSLA)** - Rosebery House, 9 Haymarket Terrace, Edinburgh EH12 5XZ. Tel: 0131 474 9200. www.cosla.gov.uk for general local government careers information.

## Related careers

Banking

Building society work

Credit control

National Health Service administration

Insurance

---

# Emma Turner
## Manager, accounts reconciliation team – HM Revenue and Customs (HMRC)

---

Emma entered HMRC with A levels and has progressed rapidly to C2 grade, which is equivalent to higher executive officer elsewhere in the Civil Service. She volunteered to take part in this book 'to make a point to all those people who said I should have gone to university'.

Plenty of careers information and advice was available at her comprehensive school in Littlehampton, she says. But as she was interested in primary teaching she put her effort into attending higher education fairs and university open days. Consequently, when she received her A level results – two Ds in English literature and history, which were not high enough for her first choice of college – she had little idea about the alternatives available. 'I could have got a place at another university or college but I had already been having doubts. I knew that teaching requires one hundred per cent commitment and felt that to go ahead without being totally certain would be to waste a place someone else could have taken. Not getting my first choice made me focus on what I really wanted to do.'

## Temporary measures

Emma didn't know what she wanted, though, and so took a temporary job in an accountant's office to earn some money and give herself time to look around. Five months later she heard through a friend temporarily employed at the local HMRC office that they were looking for more temporary staff. She looked into it and was successful in gaining a temporary post in the stamp office in Worthing. The stamp office deals with payments of stamp duty on the purchase and sale of property, stocks and shares. Emma's work consisted of the 'most basic clerical tasks – filing, opening and sorting the post and taking some phone calls.' After three months she was offered a permanent contract.

Emma stayed at the stamp office for three years, during which time she progressed from administrative-assistant level to administrative officer – inputting accounting data onto the computer, checking and preparing cheques for sending to the bank, and preparing documents for assessing. Then came her big chance.

## The big step

'My manager told me that I was ready for promotion and advised me to leave the stamp office and apply to be an executive officer at the financial accounting office in Worthing. He could have kept me there a bit longer and not had to recruit to fill my post! But he said that although he would be sorry to lose me it was the right time to make a move.'

The move was not automatic. Emma had to go through a searching application procedure. 'It was competence based. First, I had to complete a detailed application form listing my skills and competencies and giving examples of how I had demonstrated these in my work. After being successful on the first stage I had a 45-minute interview with four people. Each one asked me about the different competencies I had written about in order to reach a judgement as to whether I would be suitable. I was nervous of course, but they were very nice and helped me to relax.'

Emma was successful and moved to the financial accounting office to begin work as a band D or executive officer. She remained a band D for just under two years in a post that involved supervising a small section of five people who performed cashiering duties. Emma also had casework of her own to do relating to pension funds.

Last year she was promoted to her present job – a big step. She has a team of four staff to manage – three band D grade and one administrative officer, some of whom are much older than she is. (She is still only 24. Some of the staff are in their 50s.) The work involves supervising the reconciliation of the accounts of all HMRC's tax offices relating to running costs and staff matters. 'We are dealing with the costs of running tax offices – rent, office furniture and equipment, staffing costs, payroll, etc. We have ledgers on our computers and list every single office's expenditure under different codes. We see what has been bought in, paid out and check the information to an independent balance statement. It is rather like the reconciliation work done by accountants in private practice in making sure that their clients' accounts can be supported by evidence – except that rather than check an individual's bank account figures and cheque stubs, Emma's team deals with amounts of expenditure and invoices for large sums of money relating to the tax offices and some aspects of Customs and Excise and the Valuation Office Agency (an executive agency of HMRC). It is up to Emma to allocate work to her team. As she is fairly new to the job she is keeping for the moment to the plan worked out for the next few months by her predecessor. After that she might feel it necessary to introduce some changes.

## Training

Emma has received constant training throughout her time with HMRC. She has completed the Association of Accounting Technicians' exams, and attended numerous short courses ranging from health and safety to computing. She has had a personal development plan since she first became a permanent member of staff – which has been reviewed every four months with her immediate manager. 'Sometimes they suggest courses I should take; sometimes I do, especially if I have seen a relevant one advertised on the list of courses available to everyone. I have never had a request turned down.' Her most recent courses have been for newly appointed managers – five days so far and all highly participative, involving discussion and role-play situations. Emma is now in the position where she will have to guide the career development of her own staff. Emma has also had the support of existing managers who offer advice on how to deal with staffing and work-related issues.

## Career note

Students with 18+ qualifications can apply to join the Civil Service as trainee junior managers (known as executive officers in some departments). Entry is very competitive, however, and many join at the lower grade of administrative officer and work their way up through internal promotion as Emma has done. Some departments, including HMRC, recruit at junior-manager level very occasionally.

Administrative officers are recruited locally, so you should ask your Connexions/careers service for information or look in the local paper for advertisements. You can get general information from both the central Civil Service address given below, and directly from individual departments.

## Further information

www.hmrc.gov.uk

Because of the breadth of the Civil Service there is no central contact for information. You will find contacts for individual departments on the website www.careers.civil-service.gov.uk

## Related careers

Local government administration

National Health Service administration

Credit control

# Anna Bantin
## Administrative assistant (currently working in recruitment) – Foreign and Commonwealth Office

Anna passed A levels in English and media studies at a college in Hertfordshire. She had thought for some time that she would like a career in media production and fully intended to apply through UCAS for a degree in that subject.

However, she wanted to work and earn some money first – and so found a job with a national newspaper company where she worked as a receptionist, organised meetings and also assisted one of the editors from time to time. While in that job she saw a recruitment advertisement from the Foreign and Commonwealth Office (FCO) and decided to apply. At this stage her intention was to work there temporarily in the remainder of her gap year.

Anna was duly called for the first stage of the application procedure in London. This consisted of some timed multiple-choice tests of verbal and numerical reasoning. She was rather concerned that she did not answer all the questions in the time allowed – but it was not, in fact, necessary to do so.

'It is quite a lengthy process applying to the FCO and after I did the tests I had time to think and I began to get excited about the possibility of working there. I did some research on the role of the FCO and careers offered and became more interested in a permanent career there. I was particularly keen to travel and knew that I would have the opportunity to do so.'

Next came an interview, with two people who asked her questions about her previous administrative experience and her reasons for wishing to join the FCO. They also asked about various competencies. 'They wanted to know whether I could work in a team and if I could work to meet tight deadlines. I was able to use examples from my job at the newspaper group here, because we often had to support or cover for each other and work under pressure.'

Eventually Anna was offered a job as an administrative assistant or A1 and started work in the private office of the political director.

## First steps

Much of the work was routine but it was not confined to filing – as might have been the case in some departments – and it gave Anna an insight into the work of the FCO. 'Work in the department is very policy based. There is a lot of liaison work with Number 10 and with the Foreign Secretary's office. My work consisted mainly of collating briefings for the geographical departments (where staff specialise in work with different countries and regions) and preparing briefing packs for the director before he attended meetings in this country or in New York or Geneva. I also took minutes at meetings, made travel arrangements and booked flights, and I greeted visiting ministers from other countries. It was a very high-profile job. The hours were long sometimes. I started at 9am, but the work usually hotted up in the afternoon and evening so that often I did not get away before 8pm.'

Foreign and Commonwealth Office staff receive new postings every two years, but Anna stayed longer in her first job than was usual – 'because a situation began in Afghanistan and it was felt that it would be unfair to expect a new person to deal with the work involved.' Her first move then came and she found herself doing very different work. 'I went to the consular department, which deals with problems encountered by British citizens overseas and could include kidnappings, arranged marriages or extraditions. There was a lot of documentation involved, but it was a very hands-on job and I got to meet the public.'

## Present job

Anna's next move was to her present job in human resources. 'I work in the recruitment team and as we did a lot last year I got a good deal of experience at the other side of the desk! There are two other teams to handle induction and placement. In my team we deal with applications from people applying for jobs as administrative assistants up to junior managers. An agency sends out the forms and sifts the completed ones before passing them on to us, but we do spot checks. The agency also administers the tests but the HR department sets the pass marks. We also check references, organise selection interviews and arrange medical examinations and security checks. The applicants fill in security forms, which we pass to the vetting unit. This is the longest part of the application process. Finally, we tell candidates that they have been successful and draw up contracts.

I also help to administer work experience schemes for school and university students. I do their security clearance, introduce them to the work of the FCO – and usually visit them during their placements.'

What does Anna enjoy about her job? 'The variety. Changing jobs regularly means that you get the chance to do something completely different. I've enjoyed all of mine so far. You also get to meet different people. Then there is the fact that you know what you do makes a difference. I also like the fact that you can advance in your career. I am about to apply for internal promotion to executive-assistant level.

On the downside the pay isn't brilliant, but most people join the FCO for different reasons. I have to admit that the chance to travel is a big attraction for me! I am about ready to consider it now.'

## Overseas

Foreign and Commonwealth Office staff normally work in at least two different departments in London and for a minimum of two years before they may apply for an overseas posting. (These are regularly advertised internally.) Anna says that she will be able to give a list of requests in order of preference, although there is no guarantee that she will get her first choice. 'I can give up to eight choices and I definitely want a hot country. Somewhere in south east Asia would particularly interest me.

It should be easy to make friends in a new place, since FCO staff already working abroad are used to looking after new arrivals. The FCO always provides accommodation for its staff overseas, which could mean sharing a flat or having one for sole occupancy. In some countries staff have to live in the Embassy compound.'

Anna will be given any language training necessary before an overseas posting – and again if she moves on to another country. 'Your need for languages depends on the level of your work. Some people's training takes place in small classes and others have one-to-one tuition from native speakers.'

## Advice from Anna

'Find out as much as you can about the FCO. And if you can, apply for a work experience placement. The scheme is specifically designed to encourage people to consider a career here.'

## Career note

The FCO has about 6,000 staff comprising members of the Diplomatic Service and the Home Civil Service. Diplomatic Service staff either work in posts overseas or in offices in London and Milton Keynes. Most of the members of the Home Civil Service remain in the UK and work alongside their Diplomatic Service colleagues in home departments and occasionally in the missions overseas. There are currently 233 missions in 145 different countries.

It is a common misconception that the FCO is staffed by white, male, middle-class Oxbridge graduates. There are now large numbers of women and ethnic-minority staff doing important jobs. All candidates have an equal chance of success as they are judged against objective standards rather than against each other.

If you were interested in applying you would need to be a British citizen, be prepared to work anywhere in the world and expect to spend around two-thirds of your working life abroad. It is possible, however, to apply to stay in London for up to ten consecutive years without loss of promotion prospects.

Recruitment is through open competition. Although many candidates have degrees, those with 18+ qualifications can apply to join the mainstream of the Diplomatic Service as an executive assistant. Minimum entry requirements for this grade are five GCSEs grades A*-C (including mathematics and English language) or equivalent.

## Further information

**The Foreign and Commonwealth Office** – Recruitment Section, Old Admiralty Building, Whitehall, London SW1A 2PA. Tel: 020 7008 0804. www.fcocareers.gov.uk

## Related careers

Work in other Civil Service departments, particularly immigration.

---

# Linda Brockwell
## Housing officer – Martlet Homes

---

Linda works for Martlet Homes, a large scale voluntary transfer landlord (LSVT), in Sussex. She explains what an LSVT is. 'Local authority tenants have the right to vote on whether they wish to remain tenants of the authority or transfer ownership of the social housing stock to a registered social landlord, a housing organisation regulated by the housing corporation. If they do the latter the association becomes their landlord and manages the properties. My employer, Martlet Homes, purchased the housing stock owned by Chichester District Council following a positive vote for the housing stock to be transferred by the council tenants.'

Linda says that she grew up knowing very little about social housing. 'My mother was brought up in privately-rented accommodation and my father in a then council house, but as a family we lived in owner-occupied houses – so I knew nothing about the social-housing sector or how it was managed.' She came into this work by accident, she says, after a number of other jobs – some of which she enjoyed for a time but none of which held any strong interest.

### Looking for the right job

'After a BTEC National qualification in business studies an administrative job seemed appropriate so I found a job in a bank. That didn't work out and I moved to insurance and worked for a company where I handled applications for new home insurance policies. My third job was in the data centre of the Sussex Police Force.' By now, Linda was beginning to feel that she lacked a sense of direction and made a complete career change. She qualified for a large goods vehicle licence and drove lorries all over Europe for three years.

Her next step was to contact an employment agency in her home town of Hastings, to look for an office job. They placed her in a housing association as an administrative assistant – and she has never looked back.

## Learning about housing

Linda began by dealing with telephone requests for repairs from tenants. She took on other administrative duties, became the team clerk for a group of housing officers and eventually ended up deputising for a housing officer who was on sick leave. She was not, however, given an increase in salary. At this point Linda had become very interested in housing, had learned a lot about the work of housing officers and felt that she would like to train for the work. She also decided that she needed a change of scene and applied successfully for a job with Chichester District Council.

## The role

Housing officers work for a number of different housing providers. Some, like Linda, work for local authorities and registered social landlords; others for property-management companies or for some universities. The duties are not always the same. Some housing officers specialise in policy and planning – identifying housing needs, developing new housing schemes or modifying existing stocks and planning slum clearance and demolition of unused properties – while others act effectively as landlords for their employers and have much more contact with tenants: attending meetings of tenants' associations, and dealing with housing applications and administration of tenancies. So the job can involve managing budgets, interviewing clients, sometimes mediating in neighbour disputes, administering rent collection and dealing with arrears, organising repair and maintenance programmes, managing evictions, attending court hearings, interpreting and implementing housing legislation, developing local authority housing policy and even managing wardens and caretakers in sheltered-housing accommodation.

## Linda's choices

Linda has worked as a *generic* housing officer – a role which involved her in visiting and inspecting empty properties, signing up new tenants and dealing with all aspects of managing properties within a designated area. However, her employer recently decided that officers would become specialists in one aspect of the work – and Linda decided to work on the rents side.

In this job she deals mainly with rent arrears. This is not as simple as it sounds! It is not merely a case of writing letters, then issuing eviction orders – although she does have to do this. Part of the rent arrears recovery process involves attending possession hearings at the County Court. She has to write reports, which her association has to approve before she can proceed with an application for an eviction. But she tries to avoid such drastic steps. 'I visit tenants who are in arrears. I know most of them well and know that most are decent people who may be struggling financially. So I aim to maximise their income where I can by pointing out any benefits they might be entitled to claim. I have acquired a good working knowledge of the system now, and derive real satisfaction if someone acts on my suggestion and obtains some money that they were not aware was available. Although tax credits have been publicised by the Inland Revenue, many people are still unaware of what tax credits are and therefore have not taken up this offer of financial assistance. There is also a specialist benefits support adviser within Martlet Homes whom I can advise people to talk to. I see eviction as a last resort. Our job is to help people to stay in their homes wherever possible.'

## Qualifying

When she started work with Chichester District Council, Linda began a Higher National Certificate course in housing studies through distance learning. This was entirely on her own initiative and she received no help with course fees or time off for study. Working entirely on your own demands great self-discipline, but Linda found the course materials and support provided very good. 'When a box full of ring binders arrived I thought 'Help'. But I soon sorted it into manageable chunks and organised a pattern of work to do for each assignment. I worked on average for eight hours a week, sometimes during a whole Saturday, at other times over several evenings. I also did some reading in my lunch hours.'

When Chichester Council tenants voted to transfer to Martlet Homes, Linda became employed by the association. 'I asked the housing director whether I might get any assistance with my tuition costs for the second year of the course. She was surprised that I was paying for myself, and not only agreed to fund me through the second year but arranged for me to be reimbursed the money I had had to pay for the first year.'

Linda then progressed to the two-year professional qualification in housing awarded by the Chartered Institute of Housing (CIH), through day release.

## What does Linda like about her job?

'I think the more I learn about the work in social housing the more I want to learn. I love it and wouldn't do any other job! The part I enjoy most is meeting different people I come into contact with, and working with other agencies to assist our tenants. The work is very varied too – which makes no two days ever the same. Then I have a good team of colleagues. I work with four other housing officers who specialise in rent and tenancy work. We work very closely together and can always ask each others' advice.'

## Career note

There are no minimum entry requirements for entry to this career. Entrants have qualifications ranging from GCSEs/S grades (A*-C/1-3) to degrees, although A levels/H grades are usual for 18 + entrants.

Linda has followed courses approved by the professional body, the Chartered Institute of Housing (CIH). If you wanted to take the HNC as she did, you would normally need to have four GCSEs/S grades at A*-C/1-3 and one A level/H grade (or a BTEC National Diploma or equivalent qualification). Pre-professional courses and Apprenticeships may be available. The CIH will provide information on the work and on the approved courses.

It is also possible to take a degree course in housing studies and to obtain NVQ level 4 while in employment. Both qualifications would give entry to the CIH professional qualification course.

## Further information

**The Chartered Institute of Housing** – Octavia House, Westwood Business Park, Westwood Way, Coventry CV4 8JP. Tel: 024 7685 1700. www.cih.org

## Related careers

Human resources manager

Local government administration

National Health Service administration

Social work

Welfare rights officer

# Tamarin Gibbs

## Personal adviser – Connexions Wiltshire and Swindon

After her GCSEs, Tamarin was keen to take up art. She spent a year on an introductory art course and retook some of her GCSEs at the same time. At the end of the year, she decided that she wanted to pursue her interest in acting instead, so took a two-year BTEC National Diploma in performing arts at college. Although Tamarin made some university applications and was invited for interviews, she got cold feet. She was concerned that her chosen course would not necessarily lead to better employment prospects and that financially, it was too much of a risk. Keen to gain employment, Tamarin worked in a range of jobs before moving into an electronic circuit manufacturing company. At first she worked on production itself but she quickly achieved promotion to training work. She studied for the Certificate in Training Practice through the Chartered Institute of Personnel and Development by day release. Whilst working in training, Tamarin started to realise that she wanted a job where she could make a difference to people's lives. She knew a careers adviser and speaking to her generated an interest in that area of work. She then saw an advertisement in the local paper for an associate adviser at Lifetime Careers Wiltshire (now Connexions Wiltshire and Swindon), based in Swindon. She sent for an application pack and completed the necessary forms.

## The selection process

Tamarin was invited for an interview and was also asked to prepare a presentation on work-based learning. For the talk, she produced slides using PowerPoint. Her efforts paid off – when it came to the interview and presentation, the selectors were impressed with the amount of trouble she had taken and the obvious interest she had in the position.

## Induction and training

Tamarin's induction lasted about three weeks. This involved introductions to the different areas of the company, people's job roles and so on. She sat in on interviews with experienced careers professionals and talked to managers about various procedures in place within the company. In 2002, Lifetime Careers took on the contract to provide services for the new Connexions service, and Tamarin's job title changed from Associate Adviser to Personal Adviser.

Much of the work remained the same but the variety of clients that used the service changed, as did the types of information, advice and guidance they required. Having now worked there for over five years, Tamarin has undertaken further training. For example, she has been on several interviewing skills courses, equal opportunities training, drug and alcohol awareness training, courses in motivational interviewing and solution-focused therapy, and an Understanding Connexions training course that was assessed by means of an assignment. Tamarin has completed the NVQ level 3 in advice and guidance and is preparing to start the NVQ level 4 in learning and development support services for children, young people and those that care for them (LDSS).

## The role

Tamarin's duties are varied. When on 'new registrant' duty, she sees young people not in employment, education or training who call into the office to discuss a variety of issues including work/training, housing, benefits and free time. Tamarin also has a caseload of young people aged 16+, that she is responsible for keeping in contact with on a regular basis to support their transition into work, training or education. In addition, she works with young people who wish to move on to an 'entry into employment' (E2E) programme. She helps the young people prepare for the programme by assessing their needs, barriers and strengths, so helping to increase their chances of success.

## Likes and dislikes

Tamarin's job satisfaction comes from helping young people overcome barriers to getting into work/training or education. On the negative side, she often finds it frustrating policing people who are on benefits.

## Tips from Tamarin

'To work in guidance, it is essential to be a people person. You have to be a good listener and very patient. You should be genuinely interested about the future of your clients.'

## The future

As mentioned, Tamarin is now planning to take the NVQ level 4 LDSS. She is also considering applying for a bursary to undertake the Qualification in Careers Guidance at the University of the West of England. Eventually, she would like to train to work more intensively with post-16 young people. She realises that this will involve a lot of hard work and study.

## Career note

Connexions is the government-funded support service for all young people aged 13 to 19 in England. Personal advisers (PAs) are employed by Connexions Partnerships and may work in a range of settings, from youth clubs to information cafés. Fully-qualified PAs may be asked to offer advice on a wide range of issues, from education and careers to relationships and health. If a PA can't help, they need to know who would be best to advise the young person.

To become a fully-qualified PA, you need the NVQ level 4 in learning, development and support services for children, young people and those who care for them, and also to undergo Connexions-specific training.

As described for Tamarin, there are jobs for staff qualified to level 3, who work alongside the level 4 qualified PAs, providing support to young people. Like Tamarin, training in the workplace will lead to NVQ level 3, and it is possible to then progress further by gaining the NVQ level 4.

Apprenticeships, open to those aged up to 25, are being developed, leading to an NVQ level 3.

Alternatively, you can take a relevant degree, or an alternative specialist qualification (such as the Qualification in Careers Guidance) and then undergo local training within a Connexions Partnership.

## Further information

**Connexions** – find links to your local Connexions Partnership through: www.connexions.gov.uk

## Related careers

Careers adviser

Counsellor

Education welfare officer

Probation officer

Social worker

Youth worker

# Chapter nine

## Creative and leisure services

### Rob Wilson
#### Photographer – Jonathan Fisher Photography

Rob has always had an interest in photography. Following his work experience in year 10 where he worked in a newspaper photographic department, Rob went on to study photography and business studies at A level. He now works as a photographer at Jonathan Fisher Photography.

### First job

'I decided early on that I didn't want to go to university as I wanted to get hands-on experience in photography. After I had finished my A levels I went to school to collect my portfolio. I saw my tutor who gave me the name of someone working at a large magazine publishing company, who had been to the school to see if anyone was interested in a job as a studio assistant. I guess it was meant to be; I called him and went down for an interview the next day. I got the job and stayed with the organisation for about two-and-a-half years.'

### Next stage

'I contacted Jon Fisher myself and he invited me to an informal interview. To begin with I worked with Jon on projects where he needed assistance, and a few months later he offered me a permanent contract. When I first started I was assisting – taking meter readings, adjusting the lights and loading films. I began working on cut-out shots (product shots on a white background), but with help and guidance I have developed my photography skills and now work on large set-up shots.

I have been working with Jon for five years now. It's brilliant working with someone who has so much experience and is always willing to help me develop my skills. It's great to turn a hobby into a career.'

## A typical day

'At the start of the day I help to plan the shooting order and set up the equipment and props. I mainly work for our publishing client who produces various magazine titles – so these shots involve small room set-ups, such as a shelf in a room or a windowsill. I light each shot to give it a pleasing atmosphere and to show off the focal point at its best. We use high-end digital cameras that are tethered to computers, so some controls are done using a computer as well as on the camera. I often have to work to tight deadlines, so I need to be well organised.'

## Advice

'I think the best way to learn is to get experience in the industry. Education and qualifications can be great for some parts of the photography industry; but it's up to the individual how they want to learn. It's important to keep your ideas fresh and stay up to date with developments in the industry; reading trade journals helps. Photography is a competitive industry; if you're looking for work keep calling photographers to show you're keen (without being pushy) and you'll get a break, just like I did.'

## Career note

The largest area of employment for professional photographers is in general practice or high street photography. The British Institute of Professional Photographers (BIPP) says 'The main source of income for most general practitioners is social photography – the formal recording of family occasions. Approximately 50% of practising photographers work in this area.' Others work in advertising, fashion, press, industrial, medical and scientific photography.

Most young people aiming at a career in photography will probably go through the traditional art-school route. In some towns, however, it is possible to find employment as a trainee in a photographic studio and work, perhaps through an Advanced Apprenticeship, for NVQ level 3 in photography, then BIPP qualifications. Your Connexions/careers service will know the local situation.

You could look for the names of photographic studios in the *BIPP Directory of Professional Photography*.

## Further information

**The Association of Photographers** – 81 Leonard Street, London EC2A 4QS. Tel: 020 7739 6669. www.the-aop.org. Provides careers information on advertising, editorial and fashion photography and holds a free careers talk in London on the last Wednesday of each month (except December).

**British Institute of Professional Photography** – Fox Talbot House, 2 Amwell End, Ware, Hertfordshire SG12 9HN. Tel: 01920 46401. www.bipp.com (send an A4 size stamped addressed envelope if requesting information).

**British Journal of Photography** – their website provides details of photography vacancies, courses and qualifications: www.bjp-online.com

## Related careers

Broadcasting/film camera operation

Graphic design

Illustration

Medical photography

Photo-journalism

Press photography

# Jake Harris
## Operations consultant – McDonald's Restaurants

Jake left school after doing A levels in design technology, maths and physics, with the intention of joining the RAF. He went through the various interview stages and was offered the position of ground technician.

'I had second thoughts about choosing a career with the RAF. I had been working part time at my nearest McDonald's restaurant for just over a year and, since joining, I had always been impressed with the commitment and dedication people had, as well as the structured training programme. I knew that many of the business managers and senior managers within the company had started as crew members, proving to me that if you had the ambition, passion and are prepared to work hard, the opportunities were there. The enthusiasm displayed by others was so infectious and prompted me to think, "Should I make a career here?" I quickly had my answer.'

## Self-motivation

Jake set out to complete the steps necessary for anyone aiming at a management position within the company. 'Initially you learn the basics in the workplace. This helps quickly to develop your personal skills such as confidence, communication and how to develop successful relationships.'

## Internal training

'The training at McDonalds is comprehensive: no matter what level or position you hold within the company there is a system to ensure ongoing development. The critical part of this, in the first stages of the company, is an observation check-list, or OCL. This involves a member of the restaurant's management team working alongside you while reviewing your performance, by a combination of on-the-job evaluation and assessment of your subject knowledge.

Observation check-lists have been developed for all stations and areas within the restaurant, as well as covering food-hygiene standards and procedures. Every employee, part time, full time or at management level, receives regular performance reviews. This clearly lays out a structure for an employee to follow to help them achieve the first rungs on the management ladder. I liked this structured approach and it gave me something tangible to aim for.'

Throughout Jake's career he has attended numerous training courses designed to give the information needed to perform each role successfully. These include IT, public presenting and negotiating skills.

## First promotion

Within 12 months of starting work with McDonald's (including his part-time job), Jake was promoted to floor manager in the restaurant where he was working. 'This was a big step and my first experience in management. A floor manager has responsibilities and goals that help drive the business forward in addition to the task of training, developing and managing other employees' performance. These responsibilities, ultimately, all have an impact on the standards achieved within the restaurant and the experience a customer receives.'

## Management positions

'The next step is to become a shift-running manager before working towards a salaried role as an assistant manager. Below this level staff are paid on an hourly basis. (This is the position at which a successful graduate would join the company.) Assistant managers are a balanced mix of graduates and internally-promoted individuals. Many salaried managers in the company started as staff members – often on a part-time basis.

Every restaurant will have a business manager and typically two, or sometimes three, assistant managers. In these roles they develop their leadership skills, learn more about teamwork, people development, marketing, business planning and the financial skills needed to run the business successfully.'

At 19, Jake became an assistant manager at the Sutton Coldfield branch. 'This provided my first opportunity to manage the business, when the business manager took a holiday. I remember this being extremely challenging, but it gave me a great insight into the level of responsibility and variety of challenges a business manager's role carries.'

At this point in his career Jake was asked to help open up a new restaurant. A month before the opening date, he went to assist the restaurant's business manager with tasks including recruiting staff, and setting up systems to ensure sales planning, stock ordering and necessary audits were correct and up to standard.

'This was a fantastic opportunity for me. The team and I put a lot of time and commitment into planning for the new restaurant carefully and thoroughly to ensure a smooth opening.'

A few months after opening the restaurant, Jake returned to the Sutton Coldfield restaurant as a first assistant manager.

## His own restaurant

Jake was promoted to run his first restaurant in Tamworth High Street at the age of 21.

'Running a successful restaurant is no walk in the park, and requires a lot of determination and commitment. The training and experience I had received so far was crucial in helping me understand the solutions to the problems in the restaurant and the opportunities that existed. At every stage of my career I had experienced and worked on different tasks in great detail as part of my goals and responsibilities. I was now in a position where I was wholly responsible for these, not just working on them.

The key to driving the business forward was to delegate tasks by setting goals and giving responsibilities to each member of the management team. This would simultaneously stretch their development and create career opportunities for others.

Restaurants typically have between 40 and 80 members of staff, including a management team appropriate to the restaurant's volume. Business managers are expected to provide the highest standards of quality, service and cleanliness to the customers. The key to growing the business is to execute a robust and consistent operation; strong community relationships and local marketing plans are also key.'

Jake ran the Tamworth restaurant for eight months before moving to a very busy drive-through restaurant with an annual turnover of over £2 million. He now had over 100 staff and managers working for him – the managers were all in their late 20s or early 30s. Did this cause any problems?

'No. Restaurants employ people of all ages from school-leaving age right through to retirement. The respect I had was hopefully earned by my hard work and leadership, given over time.'

## More promotions

His next move was to become an operations consultant, with responsibility for a group of eight restaurants in Northamptonshire. 'I was responsible for the group's results and worked predominantly with the individual business managers to help them run their restaurants effectively. This role involved consulting and developing the business managers' knowledge to improve their performance and achieve better results. This would involve regular performance feedback, restaurant audits and often just spending time working on the restaurant floor together.'

Jake did this job for just under a year, at which point he was asked to become the operations consultant for Milton Keynes. After working for a period of time in this group the opportunity arose for Jake to use his experience as an operations consultant to help support franchisees who actually own and operate McDonald's restaurants.

'This role, as a field consultant, was in many ways completely new territory for me. The strength of the relationship built between a franchisee and the field consultant is what it is all about. Building trust and honesty are vital. While there might often be differing viewpoints relating to a subject, it remains crucial to listen effectively and have open dialogue in an attempt to reach win–win situations.'

Jake, who is now 29, recently embarked upon a marketing secondment.

'When this opportunity came along, it struck me as being a fantastic chance to develop myself further and would give me extensive exposure to a specialist subject. I am able to draw upon the vast experience I have gained throughout my career and use this to help complement my new role. Secondments are one of the unique advantages of working for McDonalds. Many managers in the system have been able to experience jobs in such varied disciplines as security, human resources, training and public relations, to name but a few.'

## Career note

There are no formal entry requirements to join McDonald's at the level Jake did. All promotions are based on merit. (There is a separate fast-track scheme for graduates where they can apply to start as a trainee manager before quickly becoming an assistant manager after a number of weeks.)

## Further information

Visit the website www.mcdonalds.co.uk/pages/careers/careershome.html

## Related careers

Business management

Hotel management

Retail management

# Lindsay Currie
## Library assistant – Shepherd and Wedderburn

Lindsay left school at 16. Owing to ill health, she had few qualifications but decided to do something about that when things were back to normal. Three years later, she took and passed Highers in English and psychology. Her fascination for books meant that deciding the next step was not difficult. Lindsay decided that she 'was not a university type of person' and wanted a more practical start to her career. She moved from her home area near Stirling to Edinburgh, to take up a library assistant's job with Edinburgh City Public Libraries and enrol on the HNC in library science at Telford College.

## Public library

Lindsay's job as a library assistant covered the work everyone knows about – meeting the public, issuing books, receiving book returns, replacing them on the shelves after their loan periods – but more varied! Lindsay had not thought she would be involved in clown days, puppet shows and all the presentations and activities that the libraries organised for the school holidays. She had not rated herself as being particularly good with children, but is pleased to note 'I am a lot better now'. She was also pleasantly surprised by the travel around Edinburgh she had to do – helping out at branches around the city and observing how the libraries catered for the needs of the different communities. She describes the job as 'brilliant' because of the variety and the range of customers and queries she had to deal with.

'Working in a library for me, with my interest in books, was like a kid working in a sweet shop.'

## Specialist library

The downside was that it was only a short-term contract, and she was soon looking for another job at a time when full-time permanent jobs in the city library service were scarce. Through a colleague from one of the branch libraries she was working in, she heard of an agency recruiting for a law library; she phoned – and got the job at Shepherd and Wedderburn – one of the biggest law firms in Scotland.

Already her career is demonstrating the scope of library-assistant careers. From a hectic public library scenario, she now finds herself working with one other person running an information facility for over 300 lawyers who are based in any of the company's offices in Edinburgh, Glasgow and London. In place of the latest novels and travel books in the public library, she now manages a stock of thousands of volumes of law reports, legal journals, Acts of Parliament and the Scottish Assembly, and has learned to access major online legal databases.

Each morning begins with opening the post, which will contain a lot of legal publications that have to be filed correctly. Lindsay has to make herself familiar with all this material, as she and her colleague then prepare a daily bulletin that summarises the issues dealt with in each new batch of journals, government press releases, newspapers, etc they have received. She emails this to all the lawyers in the company, helping them keep up to date with the latest developments in the legal world. It takes around two hours every day. For the rest of the day, Lindsay's research skills are really being tested. 'I could be asked, sometimes at short notice, to look up cases illustrating particular points of law, or cases dating back to a particular period about topics that any of our lawyers are dealing with at the time. We actually have books referring back to the 15th century.'

If the company library does not carry items that someone needs for a particular case, Lindsey has to hunt for the information required. This could be on the internet, and she is grateful to Telford College for giving her a sound introduction to computer searching, which she finds invaluable now.

However, the internet cannot answer all the queries she receives. One case called for some detailed information from obscure medical journals, which she eventually tracked down in the Scottish National Library, photocopied the relevant pages and was delighted to hear later, from the lawyer responsible for the case, that they had won and that her research had been a crucial factor.

## Career prospects

Lindsay has been fascinated by both the library-assistant posts she has held so far in her career. Public libraries' appeal is the constant flow of different people with different needs, and the range of methods used to broaden the appeal and usage of the library service. Shepherd and Wedderburn is obviously more targeted to its specialist clients and requires a researched and organised response. She feels that her skill profile has broadened considerably since she started work and she can now confidently include on her CV:

- research skills
- efficient and imaginative use of the internet both to research and disseminate information
- customer service skills – ability to define and respond to the needs of each individual
- operation of appropriate classification systems for ease of access to any given item or topic.

One issue for Lindsay at the moment is that she is still on a short-term contract and would like to find a permanent job before long. She has, in addition to her enhanced CV, a number of advantages in this search.

- Membership of the Scottish Law Librarians Group – a professional body, which means that she has a network of people who might be able to help her in her job search. There are other similar groups relating to other specialist libraries.

- Awareness now that many different organisations have their own specialist library. These range through other law firms, universities, large commercial companies, especially those involved in research, political organisations, area health authorities and government bodies.

- The possibility of returning to Telford College for full-time professional librarian training.

## Lindsay's advice to would-be library assistants

'Don't be put off by what you imagine library assistants are like as people. The stereotype of a library assistant is a bookish, serious looking, boring type of person. The reality, as I have found, is totally the reverse. My colleagues at both my jobs were all, at the very least, interesting, some bizarre and others totally bonkers – but all of them really great to work with.'

## Career note

Most employers expect trainee library assistants to have five GCSEs/S grades (A*-C/1-3). For work in specialist libraries and information centres they are often expected to have A levels, Highers or equivalent.

Chartered librarians must have degrees.

## Further information

**The Chartered Institute of Library and Information Professionals** – 7 Ridgmount Street, London WC1E 7AE. Tel: 020 7255 0500. www.cilip.org.uk

## Related careers

The Civil Service

Information management

Local government administration

Museum work

Tourist information centre work

# Sam Myers
## Advertising TV production assistant – Saatchi & Saatchi

Sam Myers was one of only three leavers from his year who chose not to apply for university. He left school with A level business studies (A), general studies (B), geography (E) and English (E).

Work experience with a film production company, earlier in his school career, had helped Sam decide on his very fixed objective of working towards TV production. But luck played a part in helping him get started. He had decided, before embarking on a career, that he wanted to travel. While in Australia, he had the need, as many travellers do, to earn some money to finance his travels further. A recruitment agency placed him in a job cleaning out offices. The luck was that the offices were the Sydney HQ of the Saatchi Advertising Agency. Other jobs came up in the agency. Sam became a runner doing odd jobs on shoots and locations, and ferrying tapes around to post-production companies. Instead of continuing to travel, Sam stuck with it for nine months until his work permit ran out.

Back in the UK, Sam's CV for advertising agency work had been boosted by his experience in Sydney. He sent it to a range of agencies around the south of England before Saatchi offered him work in their facilities department in their London offices. Duties here were fairly mundane – arranging rooms for conferences, setting up audio-visual equipment and so on. Again, as with the Sydney post, promotion to the job of production assistant (PA) came along as a next step.

## The job

The stages in making a commercial are: working with the client to define their advertising concept; agreeing a budget and timescale; and agreeing a script between the creative department and the client. A director is appointed to deal with the realisation of the basic creative idea. Then the production department's responsibilities kick in. Producers deal with the project administration, analysing the script to identify venues for shoots, alerting the casting department to the casting requirements, and all the nuts and bolts associated with filming, sound recording and editing.

Sam's time is spent partly at a desk dealing with administrative aspects of production, partly on location with the shoot itself, making sure that everybody involved is at the right place at the right time with the right equipment, and then with the editing and recording facilities. Working on sets and locations gives him insight into the dos and don'ts of shooting film and video. He sees the different approaches adopted by each director he works with. He understands about budgets and music copyright issues.

When shooting is completed, the project moves into a post-production phase. Production assistants are crucially involved at this stage. Post-production includes adding of sound to the film or video – speech, music, sound effects – and editing the various takes into a coherent film sequence that conveys the intended message within the required length of time.

Many sound and editing houses are to be found in Soho, in central London, and Sam will take the projects to one of these companies to use the specialist services they provide to complete a job to the highest quality standards. In this way he gets to work with some of the finest technicians around.

There are seven production assistants at Saatchi. The head or deputy head of TV production will look at each new project and allocate a PA to it. Sam might have two or three such projects on the go at any one time so he works with different producers and directors – again learning from all of them. Projects vary in size from large budget shoots, such as one that recently had him spending a week in Prague on location, to what are known in the trade as 'adapts'. Typically these would be commercials produced for audiences abroad where all that is needed is the addition of a voiceover in English. Sam will deal with these on his own without a producer.

## Personal qualities

Sam feels that most of the job is good practical common sense. 'You need to be organised and able to keep moving between one job and another remembering exactly where you left off when you were last dealing with it. You also have to be prepared to work variable hours – often working long hours to complete a job within the required deadline. 8am to 8pm on set can be counted a short day!'

As he settled into the work Sam became increasingly confident and is now able to sort things out with the minimum of fuss. Dealing with each successive Saatchi client is different, and he has learned people skills to cope with that. He can work on his own and understand when to seek help and where to go for it.

## The future

The first year was a steep learning curve where knowledge and experience came from actually doing the job alongside experts. Later will come some more support, this time from outside the company, in the form of off-the-job training by the Institute of Practitioners in Advertising (IPA). The course is followed over two weekends, some afternoons and evenings and is completed by taking the IPA exams. One of the benefits of taking this course is that Sam will meet PAs from other agencies and learn how they work through the various problems thrown up by each job. Another, of course, is a qualification that is well recognised around the country – good for his CV in the future.

At this point. Sam is not thinking of moving on as he is really satisfied with what he is learning at Saatchi. Eventually, and ideally, his ambition is to become a producer of a live programme, such as the Saturday morning TV shows for young people. For the moment he reckons that his experience as a PA will help him on that route.

---

## Career note

Many careers in advertising are usually entered by graduates. However, if you were prepared to start at the bottom, as Sam did, you could approach advertising agencies and enquire about the possibility of applying for a job as a runner.

Advertising agency staff may work towards qualifications offered by either the Institute of Practitioners in Advertising or the Communications, Advertising and Marketing Foundation.

### Further information

**The Advertising Association** – 7th Floor North, Artillery House, 11-19 Artillery Row, London SW1P 1RT. Tel: 020 7340 1100. www.adassoc.org.uk

**The Communications, Advertising and Marketing Foundation** – Moor Hall, Cookham, Maidenhead, Berkshire, SL6 9QH. Tel: 01628 427120. www.camfoundation.com

**The Institute of Practitioners in Advertising** – 44 Belgrave Square, London SW1X 8QS. Tel: 020 7235 7020. www.ipa.co.uk

### Related careers

Charity fundraising

Event and exhibition organising

Journalism

Market research

Marketing

Public relations

# Louise Matson
## Trainee assistant manager – Shearings Hotels

Louise left school in Grimsby with A levels in law, psychology, English literature and general studies. She was holding a place to study law at Wolverhampton University, but a summer job in France caused her to change her plans.

### A summer job

'I had been on family camping holidays in France with Eurocamp for years, so had applied for a summer season job with the company. I knew what the campsite couriers did, and that the work would be hard but interesting. I enjoyed it so much that I decided not to come back!'

In order to get the job with Eurocamp Louise had to spend a day at the company's head office being interviewed and taking part in discussion groups with other applicants. 'We were given problems to discuss that all related to the work. One for example, was a list of problems – power cuts, needing to get someone to hospital, part of the campsite being flooded... We had to discuss how we would deal with each of the problems, assess their priority and put them in logical order.'

Louise was accepted and spent a season, cleaning and tidying tents between guests' departures and arrivals, showing newly-arrived guests to their tents, restocking supplies of equipment and working at reception where she answered guests' questions, dealt with any problems, and generally ensured that they enjoyed their holidays. 'The couriers got to know the local area themselves and we collected leaflets on nearby attractions, which we kept in a display at reception.' It was physically hard work, but Louise enjoyed it – so much so that she did a winter season in a ski resort.

'I found', she says 'that I really enjoyed the work and realised it was time to rethink my career choice. In particular, I enjoyed meeting lots of different people and making them happy – it was really rewarding to have such an immediate impact on people's lives. When I returned to England, I found a temporary job in a bar and thought that I might make a career in bar management. I looked on the internet for breweries that might offer training in this and found that Shearings ran a hotel management training scheme. I decided to apply for that.'

Shearings began as a coach-based company, which has now expanded its range of holidays to include hotel breaks, air-, cruise- and rail-based holidays, and owns and operates 37 of its own hotels throughout England, Wales and Scotland. Louise knew, therefore, that there would be plenty of opportunity for promotion and learning within the company – from Cornwall to the Scottish Highlands.

## Training and experience

Louise first went to the Royal Hotel in Whitby, North Yorkshire, as a trainee manager. In this position she underwent a structured training and development programme covering the administration, management and control of each department within the hotel – which is designed to equip individuals with the skills and knowledge to progress within management in the company. The programme involves individuals working in each department, carrying out all the tasks as required of the staff and supervisors within that department. There is also some project work to be completed for each module as further development. The duration of the programme is usually around 18 months depending on prior experience and ability.

At the Royal, Louise spent five months shadowing the heads of departments of housekeeping, bar, restaurant, reception and kitchen – where, with the exception of the kitchen, she also gained hands-on experience of the work. She wasn't going to be attached to the kitchen long enough, she explains, to learn how to cook to a high standard. 'I was there more to observe the work of the head chef (because if he leaves the hotel manager has to be sure that the second chef is competent to take over), and if necessary to lend a hand. I can now do breakfasts and lunches, though.'

Louise then moved to the Norbreck Hotel in Scarborough as a trainee assistant manager, where she gained more experience of administration and finance, and deputised for the general manager.

During her training period Louise kept her development file in which she detailed her training needs and how she achieved them. By the end of the period it was a large lever-arch file – which she still uses. 'I found it very useful to write down exactly how I did something and I use it now in training other staff. It's very useful to be able to look at it and think, "Yes, that's how I coped with that situation".

## Advanced Apprenticeship

After she completed her training file, and following a review by her area manager and personnel and training manager, Louise was promoted to assistant manager. She then asked if there was any further training that she could do. It was suggested that she did an Advanced Apprenticeship. Until now Louise had thought that an Apprenticeship was something that was done at the age of 16, in a craft or trade. However, when she found out more about it she was keen to embark on the Hotel and Catering Training Company's (HCTC's) Advanced Apprenticeship in hospitality supervision, which she was able to do without moving either to another employer or another hotel. The training is very similar to that which Louise did under her first training programme. She has to complete another training log and write statements to demonstrate how she has achieved the competencies listed in it. She has just two more units to complete and will then have gained an NVQ at level 3.

Louise says, 'This is an ideal qualification for anyone who wants to go into hotel general management. The programme covers the very broad sweep of the business and the varying needs of the different departments such as restaurant, housekeeping, events, reception and bookings, business administration, sales, and so on. It is certainly helping me in my work on a day-to-day basis. Through gaining in depth knowledge I can see how all the individual tasks that I perform during the day impact on each other and on the bigger picture of the hotel business. This in turn makes my work more interesting and rewarding, while giving me impetus to learn more and progress my career further.

Working in the hotel business is not a nine-to-five job, and another benefit of the Apprenticeship programme is that it fits in with my job role, making it easy to work and gain qualifications at the same time. My HCTC assessor visits me regularly, and we spend time together while she assesses what I have learned, and gives additional training. The Hotel and Catering Training Company also provides lots of support materials to make sure that I'm gaining very thorough knowledge and can access information easily. I've also recently been named UK Reception Apprentice of the Year, which is fantastic. The award is open to Apprentices throughout England, Scotland and Wales, so the competition is very stiff. It will look good on my CV, alongside my qualifications and experience.'

# The future

Louise has now been at the Norbreck for two-and-a-half years and feels ready for another move. She would like to look for an assistant manager's position in another Shearings Hotel, possibly a bigger one or just one that has different types of guests. The Norbreck can receive 92 guests – who are all on Shearings coach or self-drive holidays. In a different hotel she will be able to gain experience of looking after people on different breaks, such as walking, all-inclusive holidays, or attending special events.

# Advice from Louise

'I could have done a degree or diploma course in hospitality management and I would have come out very well qualified – but nothing prepares you for the work like actually doing it. I would have learned what to do in a fire, for instance, or first aid, but I wouldn't have experienced the reality of having a guest die of a heart attack. That was a horrible experience but I coped with it.

Training the way I have chosen, I am gaining qualifications and work experience simultaneously, which is ideal. It means that I can use a practical approach that is good for the business, while I have the theory and background to back up my actions. I am thinking about doing a degree or Higher National Diploma now – but only if I can find a suitable part-time route.'

# Career note

Although it is more usual to enter the hospitality sector with applied A levels or a vocational diploma, it can be done from non-related subjects as Louise's route proves. An employer would expect you to have some suitable work experience, however.

# Further information

**The Hotel and Catering Training Company** – has regional offices in London, the Midlands, North East, North West, South East, South West, Wales and Scotland. You can find their contact details and addresses from their website: www.hctc.co.uk

# Related careers

Exhibition and events management

Pub management

Restaurant management

Tour management

# Craig Cotterill
## Corporate events manager – Alton Towers Park

Craig was always interested in catering and hospitality, but kept his options open at the A level stage. He took maths, geography and English and, although he realised that he could go to university to take a degree in hospitality management, he felt that the practical side of a college course would suit him better than formal lectures, etc.

So, with catering in mind, Craig took a City and Guilds qualification at his local college. Once he qualified, he found work in a large hotel restaurant. Here he received an excellent grounding in catering. When the business shut, Craig looked into working elsewhere.

## Selection and induction

Craig attended an Alton Towers Park 'road show' where he was able to look around to see which department interested him. He was sure he wanted to work in a restaurant, so filled in an application form and had an informal interview.

Craig started off as a seasonal member of staff at Alton Towers Park. Once on board, he attended an Alton Towers Park 'delivering the magic' induction programme. These programmes give new staff a sound introduction to the organisation, company policies and procedures, and health and safety awareness, as well as the chance to meet the rest of the team. Entertainment was provided to give some light relief from the training.

## Training and promotion

Craig's first job was as a seasonal chef in one of the restaurants in the Park. He was soon appointed unit manager in charge of the chefs and the front-of-house staff. During his time at Alton Towers Park, Craig has undertaken a wide range of training and achieved promotion as a result. He has taken hygiene certificates and has undergone licensee training. Craig's last promotion was to corporate events manager. He recently attended a two-week management training course and has gone on various short courses in people management, employment law, etc.

## Current role

As area manager for corporate events, Craig is responsible for around 60 members of staff. He has operational responsibility for all the restaurants on site, and for the many events that are held at Alton Towers Park. He holds daily team briefings to inform staff about what they can expect to happen each day, e.g. how many people are due for an event. He checks that standards are met and that the ordering process runs smoothly. Craig feels that it is important to ensure that the managers and staff are motivated to provide a good service.

For the past two years, Alton Towers Park has hosted a major corporate event for the long-serving staff of a large telecommunications company. Craig had overall responsibility for overseeing the catering arrangements for over 1,500 people. So far, the events have gone very smoothly and Craig has been given lots of compliments.

Craig really enjoys working with the people at Alton Towers Park and he finds the atmosphere a pleasant working environment. He believes that this more than makes up for the pay, which is not as high as in some areas of the industry.

## Tips from Craig

Craig says that although you can be taught a lot at college, it's only when you start working that you really start to learn. He advises people to get in at the deep end and to find a job that offers training, where the managers have a positive attitude to your career advancement!

Finally, looking to the future, Craig's big ambition is to set up his own restaurant.

## Career note

It is possible to enter the hospitality sector at all levels – from Apprenticeship to degree. Some people, like Craig, enter with A levels.

See also the career profile of Louise Matson, page 128.

## Further information

**The Hotel and Catering Training Company** – has regional offices in London, the Midlands, North East, North West, South East, South West, Wales and Scotland. You can find their contact details and addresses from their website: www.hctc.co.uk

## Related careers

Exhibition and events management

Hotel management

Pub management

Restaurant management

Tour management

# Chapter ten

# Finance and insurance

See also the profile of Lynn Elliott, in Chapter eight.

## Will McAlpine
### Acting branch manager – Skipton Building Society

Will, who has A levels in English language, media studies and law, gained at sixth form college in Taunton, is running the Skipton Building Society's branch in Bournemouth. 'I was put in here as a caretaker manager' he says, 'because I had worked in that role already and knew how to do the job. Next month I have an interview for the position of manager here.'

As branch manager Will is responsible for managing, developing and training a staff of three full-time and one part-time customer service advisers, for increasing the branch profits and for doing mortgage interviews. He also sells some financial products – general and life insurance. (An independent financial adviser is also based in the branch to offer customers specialist advice on other savings and investment products.)

### The day

Will's day normally starts at 8.10am when he arrives at the branch, ahead of the staff who come in at 8.40am. He always holds a staff meeting as soon as everyone is in to review the previous day's business, discuss which customer service adviser will be doing which tasks, and setting targets to be achieved that day in terms of sales by himself and appointments generated for him or the financial adviser by the other staff. His day then falls into one of two patterns – a mortgage-appointments day or a staff-management day.

'I generally spend an hour to an hour-and-a-half on each appointment. I have to establish a rapport with the customer quickly, and find out a lot of facts before agreeing to offer a mortgage and recommending a particular type. We have 12 different mortgages to offer, including capped, fixed-rate and tracker ones. Quite often the customer doesn't know about the different types. They just come in and ask to borrow a sum of money. After agreeing the mortgage I then offer advice on life assurance and general insurance and tell the customer what evidence of income I will need to see. Pay slips and bank statements are the usual ones. When I have these I send them up to our head office in Skipton, North Yorkshire, where the mortgage is underwritten and officially set up.

'Staff-management days are when I train staff and coach them if necessary to help them do a part of their job more successfully. I hold weekly individual meetings with each customer service adviser when I discuss their progress with them. I also observe their interaction with customers at the counter and listen to some telephone sales calls. They have a target of generating two appointments each week for me, and two for the financial adviser. If they meet these the branch achieves its target and everyone gets a bonus. It is my job to train the staff so that they can earn as much as possible! If someone has not met the target I try to find out why. If they are holding conversations with customers but not generating appointments, are they perhaps not asking the right questions? Are they not listening closely enough to the answers? If it has been a quiet week, with few customers coming in to the branch, are we doing enough to generate more business by calling customers who already have mortgages with us to tell them about other services we could offer them? When I have identified the problem I show them myself how to hold the conversation. I really, really enjoy seeing someone doing something that they had not been able to do an hour ago!'

## Getting there

Building society management was not Will's first choice of career. He first thought of doing a law degree and becoming a solicitor until he did some work experience in a solicitor's office and decided it was not the right kind of job for his personality. 'I knew that I would be more suited to a sales-type environment.' Following 'not brilliant' A level results, university was not on the cards anyway and Will took a series of temporary administrative jobs while trying to work out what to do. In the last one – in a supermarket where he was working very long hours for very poor pay, he was becoming depressed and realised that he had to move when his girlfriend, who worked in a different building society in Taunton, told him that she had seen an advertisement for a trainee customer service adviser in the window of the Skipton branch. Will knew a little about the work through her, decided to apply for the job and got it.

## Training

All Will's training was delivered by the branch manager and by other colleagues. He spent a short period sitting by a colleague and observing, learned about all the different products and services, then soon moved on to dealing with customers on his own – but with his manager or a senior colleague sitting beside him at first. 'There is no substitute for doing the job yourself', he says. 'It's the quickest way to learn – but of course you can't be allowed to make mistakes, so supervision is essential at first.'

Will soon decided that if he wanted to progress he would need to acquire some professional qualifications, and enrolled on a distance-learning course leading to the Certificate in Mortgage Advice Practice (CeMAP), awarded by the Institute of Financial Services/Chartered Institute of Bankers. His manager was unable to fund the course for him, but she was generous with study time and managed to give him several hours most weeks. He was within two months of completing the course when he saw the position of area mortgage adviser advertised and asked his manager if she thought he could do that job. She advised him to apply for it, and 18 months after joining the Society, Will achieved his first promotion.

## Mortgage advice and branch management

The new job had been created because the branches in Bristol and Plymouth were particularly successful in generating business, so much so that the two managers would have spent all their time on mortgage interviews and none on staff management. Furthermore, the Bristol branch was without a manager. Will took over the mortgage work, spending three days each week in Bristol and two in Plymouth.

He had been doing this for five months when his regional manager asked him if he would like to become the acting branch manager in Bristol. 'They knew I could sell, but they had no idea whether or not I could manage people. So I was given the job and given six months to prove myself. Before I started I attended a two-week course in Skipton, with other new branch managers. It was a really good course.'

## A tough decision

At the end of the six months Will's regional manager offered him an interview for the permanent job of branch manager at Bristol. Will now had a very difficult decision to make. He had spent a holiday in Spain with his brother who owned a bar there and fallen in love with the country. His brother offered to employ him in the bar, and Will agonised over losing a fantastic opportunity with the Skipton. He finally decided that if he did not go to Spain he would always regret it, and explained his decision to the regional manager who was very understanding.

However, four months in Spain were enough to show Will that he needed a job with more challenges. He returned to England and rang his former regional manager to enquire about the possibility of working for the Skipton again. The manager of the Bournemouth branch had just left and Will was immediately offered the acting manager position for three months.

## The future

Within five years Will would like to be in a regional manager's job, with responsibility for several branches. After that the promotion opportunities could include becoming head of branch development or moving to take up a post at head office.

## Career note

Building society staff now share a common series of professional exams run by the Institute of Financial Services or by the Chartered Institute of Bankers in Scotland. To gain an Associateship of the Institute in England and Wales candidates follow an approved course based on its own material, which is reviewed by Manchester University and leads also to a BSc in financial services. The Scottish Institute goes for distance-learning training supplemented by a higher-level course taken on block release to university.

## Further information

**The Building Societies Association** – 3 Savile Row, London W1S 3PB. Tel: 020 7437 0655. www.bsa.org.uk

**Financial Services Skills Council** – 51 Gresham Street, London EC2V 7HQ. Tel: 020 7216 7366. www.fssc.org

**The Institute of Financial Services** – IFS House, 4-9 Burgate Lane, Canterbury, Kent CT1 2XJ. Tel: 01227 762600. www.ifslearning.com

**The Chartered Institute of Bankers in Scotland** – Drumsheugh House, 38B Drumsheugh Gardens, Edinburgh EH3 7SW. Tel: 0131 473 7777. www.ciobs.org.uk

## Related careers

Accountancy

Banking

Independent financial advisory work

Insurance broking

# Darren Fagan
## Senior business manager – NatWest

Darren works in the business centre of the NatWest branch in Winchester, Hampshire, where he looks after the interests of 150 local businesses each with a turnover of between £200,000 and £2 million. At 26 Darren is forging a very successful career. He is the youngest business manager in the region to be responsible for £14 million of the bank's assets. Yet he had never considered a financial career until a friend suggested business banking to him!

### Current role

Darren provides a range of financial services to his customers. He conducts financial reviews, deals with any queries and problems – often anticipating problems that might arise and planning how to deal with them, and authorises loans when the applications are made. Any one of his clients might wish to borrow sums ranging from £50,000 to £1.5 million.

'I plan my own week with my assistant who controls the diary. We decide our targets and aim each week for a balance between appointments with existing customers – to review our services and performance and find out whether we can help them in any other way – and appointments with potential new ones. This is a very competitive business. Other banks are also targeting my customers, so I have to be able to prove that I can offer something better. By that I don't just mean ability to undercut fees. I don't want customers who are simply rate driven. If businesses move to me simply in order to save money they will leave as soon as a cheaper offer is made. They must be service driven. I aim to keep their loyalty. I encourage all my customers to keep me informed if they anticipate problems – for example, late payments or unpaid bills that could cause cash-flow problems. I can then probably arrange to cover the gap, whereas if they don't tell me, their accounts will be short of funds and cheques that they write could bounce. All my customers have my email address and my mobile phone number and I will even take phone calls in the evenings.

As I said, part of my role is to find new customers. One way of doing this is to regard all my existing customers as potential introducers. Every time I visit one I ask before leaving if there is anyone they could recommend me to. I'm also a member of a local networking club or business referral exchange. It is a group of individual professionals – financial advisers, solicitors and accountants – who meet for breakfast at 7.15am once a week. We explain our roles to each other and exchange business cards. I go partly to look for new business, but more to meet with the city's movers and shakers and keep abreast of what is happening.

Another way of getting my and the bank's name known is to support community initiatives. I recently agreed to sponsor a rugby tournament for 800 boys. There were a lot of parents there who might be business owners. I also agreed to pay for the programmes for an event one of my customers was organising. And just last week I gave a presentation and ran a question and answer session on student finance in a sixth form college. All these activities help to create good will.'

## Making a career choice

Darren left his 11-16 school, Westgate, in Winchester, and went to nearby Andover College to do an Advanced GNVQ in leisure and tourism (now an applied A level). He left there – and 'more interested in moving in with my girlfriend than establishing a career' found a job as an assistant manager with a high street baker's shop. (He was recruited at that level as he had experience of working in a motorway service station.)

'A friend from college who had done the business studies course there told me that I was wasted where I was and suggested that I would enjoy banking, which was what he was doing. On his advice I applied for a job with the NatWest in Piccadilly, London. The application process was a lot less complex than it is now, with most applicants attending assessment centres. I went for an interview with the area business manager who asked me fairly standard questions. He also read my CV and asked me quite a bit about my experience and skills in customer service. A week later I received a letter offering me a job as a small business assistant.'

## Career moves

'I did this job for six months and then was promoted to the job of small business adviser. I enjoyed this work very much. My GNVQ was not as irrelevant as it might sound because it is very much an applied business course, with modules in accounts, management and marketing – but all relevant to the leisure industry. Our definition of a small business is a start-up, or one that has low credit value – that is, will not need to borrow very much.

I then became a senior business assistant, looking after 250 higher-value clients and providing one-to-one support for a senior business manager. I did this role for 18 months then was promoted to a small business manager, with 2,500 low-value clients to look after. Most of my clients were travel agents. There were about 700 of them, with five or six new ones opening up each week.

I liked the work and I enjoyed being in central London. It meant a long journey every day, though, and after nearly three years I decided to work nearer to Winchester. By now I was married and had small children who I wanted to spend more time with.

There were no immediate vacant positions in business management, but I attended an assessment centre to find out what roles I might be regarded as capable of. It was interesting. I had to give a presentation on how I would improve an underperforming portfolio, role play in a customer service situation, and attend one-to-one interviews. Soon afterwards I was contacted and offered a job here in Winchester as a customer adviser. I decided to take it in order to gain some different experience and, of course, because it was in the branch I wanted to work in. I'm glad that I did. I was in a bigger team, there was more variety of work (I was advising on products like mortgages and investments), and I learned a lot about how the branch works. I decided now to carve out a serious career plan, achieve all my targets and gain a good reputation so that I would be noticed and earmarked for promotion. Three years later a vacancy came up in the business centre – and I got the job.'

## A move to the business centre

'I became a manager for medium-sized businesses and I had a full-time assistant working for me. I had been out of business work, of course, while in customer service, so I had to work hard to bring myself up to speed quickly. I spent some time visiting customers with my manager to learn from him and also made some visits on my own – to introduce myself and to familiarise myself with their businesses. In just under a year I was promoted to my present position.'

In addition to his main role as a senior business manager, Darren has a second one as area franchise manager. The bank has 20 throughout the country. A lot of people don't realise it, but many high-street companies are run by franchisees, people who buy the right to run them, using the company logo and equipment following a common plan made by the franchiser. Many fast-food outlets are run like this. So are some playgroups, activity centres, office suppliers, cleaning companies and car rental businesses. Darren says 'NatWest is the market leader in franchise banking. We have a number of clients who are franchisers – the companies who sell franchises. They refer their franchisees to us and we deal with their day-to-day banking needs.'

## Training

All Darren's training has been conducted by the bank. As a specialist, he has not been required to take the Institute of Financial Services' examinations, which colleagues aiming for branch management (and higher posts in retail banking) would need to do. He has trained for each of his different jobs by learning from more experienced managers, and by observing for himself how the work is conducted. 'You can learn more from ten customer visits than from any textbook!' He has also attended short courses from time to time, on topics such as customer service, credit lending, negotiating and managing people.

## What does Darren enjoy about his job?

'Everything. I like getting to know businesses really well and providing them with a good service. I like the variety. And I like the fact that as long as I deliver I am left alone to get on with and develop my job. In customer service you are micro-managed, that is your manager will ask you how every customer interview went and what you achieved. I see my manager once or twice a month.'

## Darren's advice

'If you would like to get into a particular area of banking I would suggest getting a job in a branch in any role and at any level. Then – make your own opportunities. Show enthusiasm, learn about the job you really want to do, and get yourself known by managers. Area managers keep progression lists that show who can be recommended for promotion or for transfer to a different job.'

## Career note

Work in banks has changed a good deal over recent years. The number of positions in retail branches for cashiers or counter assistants has decreased, while those in customer service and telephone-banking service have increased. Your local Connexions/careers service will know which opportunities exist in your area.

If you were hoping to become the overall manager of a branch it would be necessary to study for the examinations of the Institute of Financial Services (IFS) England, or the Chartered Institute of Bankers' (CIOBS) examinations in Scotland.

## Further information

Information about careers in banking can be obtained from local branches or from the regional office of any of the banks.

**The Institute of Financial Services** – IFS House, 4-9 Burgate Lane, Canterbury, Kent CT1 2XJ. Tel: 01227 762600. www.ifslearning.com

**The Chartered Institute of Bankers in Scotland** – Drumsheugh House, 38B Drumsheugh Gardens, Edinburgh EH3 7SW. Tel: 0131 473 7777. www.ciobs.org.uk

## Related careers

Accountancy

Banking

Independent financial advisory work

Insurance broking

# Fiona Catling
## Semi-senior accounting technician – Hayles, Farrar & Partners

Fiona gained A levels in maths, chemistry, physics and psychology – chosen, she says, because she had no career ideas at the time, and so chose three subjects that she enjoyed and that would also open many doors. Psychology, she added, because she also wanted to study something new. She particularly enjoyed maths, but despite her maths teacher suggesting university she knew that she wanted to go straight into a career. It took a little while to decide what to do but after several discussions with her maths teacher and with a careers adviser, both of whom were very helpful, she settled on accountancy and made several job applications.

She is now working for accountancy firm Hayles, Farrar and Partners in Leicester and thoroughly enjoying a varied role within the company. She has just finished the technician level (NVQ level 4) of the Association of Accounting Technicians' (AAT) accounting qualification. She was allowed to start at the intermediate level – a level 3 qualification rather than the foundation level – as she already had A levels. Study for the qualification, she says, was not a big jump from A level work as they were both level 3 qualifications. Her particular subjects had taught her to solve problems in a logical way, and even exempted her from the first level of the AAT exams.

## Career decision

Fiona decided to train in an accountancy firm rather than in industry or the public sector, and chose to take the AAT route because she knew that the qualification was accepted as an entry point by the professional bodies in both chartered and certified accountancy should she wish to train eventually to become a fully-qualified professional accountant. She sent letters of application with a CV to 12 firms and received replies from them all. The ones that had no vacancies all offered to keep her details on file and she had three interviews, all of which resulted in offers of jobs. She accepted the one from Hayles, Farrar and Partners because she had liked the atmosphere when she went for interview, and because she had heard that the firm had a reputation for offering good training.

## Work with clients

The firm has a range of clients, from self-employed individuals who require assistance in completing their annual tax returns, to limited companies whose tax affairs are more complicated. Fiona started work on real accounts straight away, working on individual clients' records of income and expenditure. Her job was to prepare the accounts and put them in the right format for the Inland Revenue. She had to go through clients' own records, checking their income and expenditure, making sure that they had receipts to back up expenditure claims, check their VAT receipts and doing reconciliations (ensuring that the figures on cheque-book stubs balanced with the bills claimed as paid). Some were relatively easy because the clients kept detailed lists and could produce all the evidence required, whereas others sent in bundles of invoices, VAT forms, receipts and bank statements in no particular order – with numbers of receipts missing. This would mean phone calls to find the information. When she had all the information she needed she would work out which allowances clients could legally claim and how much tax they would have to pay. Fiona was trained for this work by senior colleagues who would check her work – and right from the beginning she was allowed to work on accounts from start to finish.

Quite soon after joining the firm, Fiona also went out on audit. Audits are a legal requirement for companies with annual turnovers above a certain limit. An audit team from the company's accountants visits their premises, carrying out work to make sure that the accounts are accurate. It is work that involves checking invoices and receipts – just as with the individual clients – but might also for example, involve writing to a sample of people who are listed as owing the company money and in some cases checking physically that stock listed does exist. The audit team normally also interviews the company's accounts staff and some managers. During the first two years Fiona went as a junior member of the team and was given tasks to do by the lead auditor. She will soon be going as the lead auditor and taking a junior with her.

How do the clients react to Fiona? 'Some do think I am rather young, and some insist on seeing a qualified accountant. But most can see that I know my job and respect me.'

## Qualifying

Throughout her training Fiona has been given day release to attend courses run by the Financial Training Company in Leicester, where she prepared for the AAT exams with technicians from other accountancy firms. She found both the course content and the tuition very good. The AAT course materials covered everything she needed to know and the tutors were always available to assist – 'they gave me their home phone numbers and email addresses'.

## The future

Although she could have a satisfying career as a technician, Fiona has decided to qualify as an accountant and has opted for the certified accountancy qualification. Her AAT qualification gives her two exemptions, and if she passes every exam at the first attempt she will be a fully-qualified accountant at the age of 22.

To sum up, Fiona says 'I know a lot more now than I would have if I had come out of university having done an accountancy degree. We have had staff who came from university and staff starting after A levels, but the people who have done the AAT accounting qualification are able to do things much more quickly. The main difference for me was being taught in a work environment, rather than learning the theory in isolation. Being able to apply on a daily basis what I was learning on the AAT course was far more useful. I'm working. I'm enjoying it and I'm earning money, instead of going to university and ending up in debt three years later.'

## Advice from Fiona

'If you decide on the employment route after A levels, see a careers adviser as soon as possible and start to get some ideas together. Spend time writing a good CV and have it ready to send to prospective employers.'

## Career note

Accounting technicians study for the qualification of the Association of Accounting Technicians (AAT) as Fiona is doing, or through ACCA, which also offers a training scheme. There are no formal entry requirements but entrants are expected to have a reasonable standard of numeracy and literacy.

Through the AAT scheme trainees work towards either NVQ/SVQs levels 1-4 in accounting or for the AAT's own diploma. These are of equal standard and both are competence-based. Some employers support students through day-release or in-house training. Evening classes and a distance-learning method are also available. It is possible to train through an Advanced Apprenticeship. Qualified accounting technicians can go on to become qualified accountants and are granted exemption from some of the first-level professional examinations.

## Further information

**The Association of Accounting Technicians** – 154 Clerkenwell Road, London EC1R 5AD. Tel: 020 7837 8600. www.aat.co.uk

**The Association of Chartered Certified Accountants** – 2 Central Quay, 89 Hydepark Street, Glasgow G3 8BW. Tel: 0141 582 2000. www.acca.org.uk

## Related careers

Independent financial advisory work

Insurance underwriting

Tax advisory work

Tax inspection

# Justin Randall
## Financial adviser, Asset Management, Independent Financial Advisers Ltd

Independent financial advisers (IFAs) work with clients to find financial products that suit their needs. A client could be one person, an organisation, or a group of individuals. The sorts of products they advise on may include pensions and savings plans, mortgages, investments, life insurance and critical illness cover, income protection and medical insurance.

Justin, who left St Vincent's Sixth Form College in Gosport, Hampshire, with A levels in English language and communication studies, works at Asset Management in Southampton. The firm has seven other registered advisers plus support staff. It is, says Justin, a small regional firm of independent financial advisers with a varied list of clients. Most are individuals of high net worth; there are also self-employed people – all introduced by other professionals like their accountants – and a number of group pension schemes.

Justin came into this career 'by accident'. He was intending to become a journalist (which explains his choice of A level subjects) but on leaving college took a stop-gap job with an insurance company, and enjoyed it so much that he stayed. 'I started in sales support in the independent financial advice division, inputting details of new business into the computer system.

There is a lot of networking in this industry. You meet people from other branches – banking, accountancy, insurance and so on – through your work. I was offered a job here after talking to one of the directors who knew that I was working on a project that was of interest to them.

Asset intended to bring me on as a financial adviser, so I started work in the role of paraplanner. (Paraplanners provide administrative support to financial sales people.) As assistant to one of the directors I did research, wrote reports, arranged quotations and did day-to-day administration. I then became an IFA myself.

Independent financial advisers do portfolio planning for individual clients. After making the initial recommendations they review their portfolios annually and may make suggestions for revisions. You need to understand your clients' needs and attitudes very well indeed. This applies equally to an individual or an organisation. Their requirements can be very different. They might need advice on one particular method of saving, for example – for a wedding, for school fees, retirement income; they might want to plan for inheritance tax avoidance; or they might want to invest in shares through ISAs.

I always meet a client face to face and go through some very detailed questions with them. I need to establish their current financial situation, their attitude to risk, any preferred form of investment and any they wish to avoid, before I can give any advice. There is a set of questions that we use. Then we make a stochastic model and produce some model portfolios. The stochastic model means feeding in various permutations of factors such as stock-market crashes, changes of government, a client's wish not to invest in certain countries... It is a scientific way of investigating options, but you certainly do not need A level maths.

When you have all the possible options you explain them to the client and make sure that they have understood everything. You then take their instructions to proceed.'

## Current job

'I now do less work involving client contact because a project I am working on takes up most of my time. It has grown out of the work I was doing at the insurance company – and is one of the reasons Asset offered me a job. 'Wrap' is a system that is in use in Australia and the USA but is very new here. Basically, it involves aggregating a client's holdings in one place. You have a bit more control that way – and everything is more easily accessed and managed online. The software house that set up one particular Wrap scheme in this country did some research and identified eight financial advice firms that were truly independent – that is, not tied to any insurance company or bank – and invited them to become founder members. Asset Management was one of them, and as I had been developing a similar scheme for the insurance company I set up a technical team here to implement it. It is now almost up and running and we shall move most clients over to it in the next three years.'

## Qualifications

Justin had already obtained the Certificate in financial planning while working in insurance. He did more study a year ago. 'Last year saw the biggest shake up in pensions legislation in our generation. I took a specialist pensions exam in order to be up to speed. I did this in my own time through distance learning. I shall now take some more specialist qualifications.'

## The pluses

What does Jason enjoy about his work? 'The sheer variety. No two clients are the same. You could be helping a young couple wanting a mortgage, followed by a company director making a huge pension investment. And I like the pace of work, which is very fast.'

## Advice from Justin

'You need to be very flexible – and prepared to work flat out when necessary. The six weeks leading up the end of the financial year, for instance, are hectic and everyone is stretched. The summer is quieter – then everyone starts to think about their finances again in September.

I would advise anyone coming into the industry to try to establish what their specialist interest is as early as possible. You can be a generalist or a specialist in this job. I worked first as a generalist, and it took me a while to work out where my interests really lay. Because of that I didn't start working for specialist exams until fairly recently. Because I now want to gain more qualifications in pensions, I estimate that I shall be doing part-time study for about four years.'

## Career note

Financial advisers work either as tied advisers, recommending only products marketed by their own organisations, semi-tied, with links to more than one, or, like Justin and his colleagues, as independent advisers, who advise on the products available from a range of financial organisations.

Each organisation will supply training in its own products, normally a combination of formal tuition and on-the-job experience supervised by senior advisers. Trainees will also be required to undertake recognised industry training, regulated by the Financial Services Authority.

## Further information

**Association of Independent Financial Advisers** – Austin Friars House, 2-6 Austin Friars, London EC2N 2HD. Tel: 020 7628 1287. www.aifa.net

**The Chartered Insurance Institute** – 42-48 High Road, South Woodford, London E18 2JP. Tel: 020 8989 8464. www.cii.co.uk

**Financial Services Skills Council** – 51 Gresham Street, London EC2V 7HQ. Tel: 020 7216 7366. www.fssc.org

**Institute of Financial Planning** – Whitefriars Centre, Lewins Mead, Bristol BS1 2NT. Tel: 0117 945 2470. www.financialplanning.org.uk

**Institute of Financial Services** – IFS House, 4-9 Burgate Lane, Canterbury, Kent CT1 2XJ. Tel: 01227 762600. www.ifslearning.com

## Related careers

Accountancy

Insurance broking

Insurance underwriting

Investment analysis

Pensions management

# Sally Parker
## Compliance analyst – Skipton Building Society

Sally took her A levels – in maths, physics, chemistry, art and general studies at South Craven Comprehensive School in North Yorkshire. While there she put in a UCAS application 'to keep everyone else happy – but without any real intention of going to university', and chose to apply for English and philosophy! 'Not surprisingly', she says, 'I wasn't offered any places – but I was offered engineering.'

When the results came out Sally's grades were lower than predicted, but she was not too concerned. She had found an administrative job as soon as the exams finished – at the headquarters of the Skipton Building Society a few miles away. 'I had no real idea of what I wanted to do', she says, 'and so I looked for a job with a local company that would train me.'

## Starting work

Sally started in the deeds department, doing what was fairly routine administrative work, checking information required when customers were taking out mortgages. 'I would get the title deeds to the property from solicitors and had to check that all the details were there and were correct. Often they were not. Sometimes local authority searches had not been carried out, or I would ask for information on the endowment policy we had been informed the customer had taken out, only to find that it had not been organised. I spent a lot of time on the phone to solicitors, customers and life assurance companies. It was very good experience in customer service work.'

On her first day Sally went straight to her department, where she was the only new entrant. She was given all the training she needed to do her job by her supervisor and other colleagues, who taught her how to tackle tasks like policy enquiries or queries on boundary disputes. As soon as she was judged competent she joined the departmental rota and was allocated to different work each week. When she had been there a few weeks she attended an induction course of several days with new staff from other departments and from some of the branches. Managers from different departments explained their work and Sally felt that both customer relations and compliance sounded interesting.

The Society sends annual statements to customers in January. At that time extra staff are needed in customer services where a team is set up, staffed by people from other departments, to handle the additional work. Sally went to work there for two months and thoroughly enjoyed it. 'Sometimes I was in a call centre, taking telephone enquiries and sometimes I dealt with letters. I dealt with queries regarding interest on investments, mortgage payments, transfers of money from one account to another – all kinds of things. I had never dealt with investment work before, but we were given intensive training plus reference manuals and names of people we could refer to if in difficulty. I had to do quite a bit of figure work at times.' Sally felt that she was learning a lot in this department and beginning to get a feel for what really interested her – so much so that she made a move to customer services permanently. She was now handling communications from customers throughout the year. Here she gained an NVQ level 3 in customer service.

## Promotion

After about two years she was promoted to senior customer services adviser and then to supervisor. Now, she had both to manage and train other people. This might not have been easy, given that some were older than Sally and had different levels of experience. 'There was a wide range: from school leavers to mums working part time, to people who had previously held more senior jobs and were now looking for something less stressful!' She did attend some formal courses – mainly on disciplinary procedures and on how to conduct appraisals. Sally trained new entrants, arranged for her staff to make visits to other departments and also carried out quality checks on her staff's work. A great deal of diplomacy was required but Sally found that her experience in dealing with the Society's customers helped greatly. 'I think one or two people did resent my promotion, but I had learned through dealing with customers how to word things. I had made most of my mistakes already!'

## Qualifications

By now Sally felt that she needed some technical qualifications in order to progress. She was also ready to start working for exams again and enrolled for an evening class to study for Part 1 of the Financial Planning Certificate. Unfortunately, the class folded due to lack of numbers but Sally and a small number of other students formed their own study group, meeting in each others' houses, and gave each other mutual support. Since then she has also gained the Certificate in Mortgage Advice Practice (CeMAP), awarded by the Institute of Financial Services/ Chartered Institute of Bankers and the Mortgage Advice Qualification (MAQ) of the Chartered Insurance Institute.

Eighteen months later Sally moved to compliance. Here she is responsible for the work of two trainee analysts and an administrator. The job is varied, detailed – and comparatively new. It is almost, says Sally, what she makes of it, and she has developed her role since taking up the post.

Compliance means ensuring that everything the Society does meets the regulations laid down by the regulatory authority responsible for building societies, the Financial Services Authority. 'They issue the rule books and it is up to us to identify issues, interpret the rules and ask whether the Society is keeping to them. If not, how can we change our procedures? How do we monitor them and ensure that they are correct? We start the year with a compliance plan, which covers our main activities of mortgage advice, investment advice and products, but also covers other things such as data protection and any complaints from investors over the financial advice they were given. I have to look at all the likely changes to regulations and work out how we can comply with them. I then have to inform department managers and help to organise training for staff on the implications and changes that need to be made to procedures. It is not always a popular role! A balance has to be achieved between business interests and over-regulation. We are sometimes affectionately referred to as the business prevention unit! We are a good team and all have experience gained from working in other departments.'

## The future

Sally is happy in her present post and does not envisage moving in the near future. She does plan, however, to obtain more qualifications, in particular the relatively new Diploma in compliance.

## Sally's advice

'I got my first job very much by chance. I had not done much looking around. Luckily I found a job that enabled me to learn and to work out where I could go next. It opened doors for me. I would advise people to spend plenty of time looking into their options and not to feel rushed into making a decision.'

## Career note

Banks and building societies offer a variety of careers in their head offices. It is possible to join in one capacity, then experience several different jobs and gain promotion, as Sally has done.

## Further information

**The Chartered Insurance Institute** – 42-48 High Road, South Woodford, London E18 2JP. Tel: 020 8989 8464. www.cii.co.uk

**Financial Services Skills Council** – 51 Gresham Street, London EC2V 7HQ. Tel: 020 7216 7366. www.fssc.org

**The Institute of Financial Services** – IFS House, 4-9 Burgate Lane, Canterbury, Kent CT1 2XJ. Tel: 01227 762600. www.ifslearning.com

## Related careers

Banking

Independent financial advisory work

Insurance broking

# Chapter eleven

# The Services, security and law

## Heidi Schulz
### Police constable – Cheshire Constabulary

Heidi attended Runcorn Heath High School, a comprehensive school in Runcorn, Cheshire, from where she emerged with a clutch of GCSEs but no ambition for any further academic qualifications at that age. She took a job in a local factory as a machine operator making zips – and soon began to discover other skills, such as being able to get along with and influence people. She was promoted to the role of leader of a shift team of 35 people and became involved with the union as a shop steward. She had to attend conferences, negotiate with management, talk at meetings of staff and help with issues such as the company's equal opportunities policy. She gained the respect both of management and of her fellow workers.

Heidi then began to regret her comparative lack of qualifications and, having acquired an interest in law, enrolled at the local college of further education for evening classes. Eventually she passed A level law with a grade C – comfortably her best performance in education to date. There was another benefit from the law course in that some of her fellow students worked either in the local law courts or the police. From them she learned more about police work and they encouraged her to think about a radical change of career.

### Applying

She sent for the application forms for Cheshire Constabulary, and spent two weeks completing them making sure that she had researched the requirements as thoroughly as she could and that she had included all the relevant information from her experience to date.

Several months passed, during which she enrolled in a gym to 'lose weight and get myself really fit'. Then everything happened in a rush as the selection process kicked in:

- Stage one. A physical examination plus a variety of tests that made her glad she had joined the gym. Written tests in English and maths.

- Stage two. A group of those who were left were invited to a session that tested their abilities to interact with people and express themselves clearly. This included talking to a group about herself, and later being given a topic and instantly having to talk about it for two minutes. Her work in meetings at the zip factory turned out to be useful training for this.

- Stage three. This stage tested physical, communication and teamworking abilities through a series of exercises at an outdoor pursuits centre.

- Stage four. A phone call Heidi was delighted to receive, inviting her for a uniform fitting.

## Training

Cheshire Police have a training centre at Crewe where Heidi spent the first two weeks of her new career, followed by 15 weeks at a national police training centre at Bruche, near Warrington. Here, in the company of recruits from forces around the UK, she worked through a huge range of topics – powers of arrest and entry, giving evidence in court, handcuffing, self defence, life saving and first aid, and further fitness exercises. Success here was recognised by an impressive passing-out parade to which her family were invited – and a week's leave.

After another period at the Crewe training centre, Heidi finally started as a police constable at Widnes police station. The training was by no means at an end, but now took on a far more practical slant as she was allocated to a tutor officer whose job it was to steer her through the first months of 'real work' offering her support, advice, going out with her on police duties around Widnes and helping her with the mountains of paperwork her various cases threw up.

## The job

Now several months into the job, Heidi does not have to be escorted everywhere by her tutor officer but has support from him and the rest of her team at Widnes. Enthusiastically, she describes every day as offering something new – a breath of fresh air after the factory. Since starting at Widnes she has, among other things:

- been involved, with her tutor, driving in pursuit of a stolen car where the driver decamped on a housing estate before being tracked down by the two officers.

- been to a magistrate to obtain a warrant to search a house where it was suspected that a potentially dangerous psychiatric patient might be hiding. The patient was in fact under a bed and Heidi, using her communication ability and persuasive skill, managed to get him to the hospital that was dealing with him.

- assisted with violent 'domestics' helping to calm down the parties to the disputes.

- delivered the sad news of a sudden death to the distraught next of kin – a task that called for enormous tact and sympathy. The response of the bereaved person to her efforts made Heidi feel that she had been able to help someone through a very traumatic event.

- undertaken routine street patrols – really a sort of public relations job where the reassuring presence of a police officer is seen to be there and available. If crimes are seen they are dealt with, but there is also the likelihood while out on patrol that she will be called to deal with crimes or incidents that have been reported in her area.

- made arrests for a wide range of alleged offences and given evidence in court where the defendant pleads not guilty.

The downside of the work is the constant paperwork involved after an arrest in order to bring the case to court. The positive side is that Heidi is encouraged to use her own initiative as much as possible. She can be proactive and focus her work on areas of need. The station has an intelligence section, which she can use to work out any patterns of crime – where and when it is happening. From this information, she can work out places to attend when there is a strong chance of something happening.

## The future

Heidi is still learning. She still has some time to run on her initial probationary period and wants to extend her experience still further before making a decision on which direction she wants to take her police career – traffic, CID (criminal investigation department), or other specialist aspects of police work. There are police promotion exams to think about later – further opportunities to gain qualifications. In the meantime, she feels that she has made good use of her A level, and made the most of the experience of life she gained after leaving school.

## Career note

There are 52 separate police forces in the UK (plus the British Transport Police, Ministry of Defence Police and the UK Atomic Energy Authority Constabulary). Entry directly after school at 18+ is possible but not usual. Usually, recruits have some career experience between school and applying successfully for a probationary period in their chosen constabulary. The old minimum-height requirements have been abolished, but candidates obviously need to be physically fit. Eyesight requirements vary from force to force and the wearing of spectacles or contact lenses may not be a barrier, providing there is reasonable unaided vision.

## Further information

From your local force or from:

**National Police Recruitment Team** – Tel: 020 7273 3684 and 0870 000 1585. www.policecouldyou.co.uk

**Police Division** – The Scottish Executive Justice Department, St Andrew's House, Regent Road, Edinburgh EH1 3DG. Tel: 08457 741741 and 0131 244 2156. www.scotland.gov.uk

**Scottish Police Forces** – www.scottish.police.uk

**The Police Service of Northern Ireland** – The Consensia Partnership, PO Box 268, Belfast BT1 5PH. 0800 028 4411. www.psni.police.uk or www.selectnip.org

## Related careers

Firefighter

HM Forces

Prison officer

Private detective

Security guard

# Lyndsey Taggart
## Senior policy development executive, BUPA Insurance

Lyndsey works as an in-house lawyer, specialising in commercial (financial services) law and contract. She did not decide on this career, however, until well after taking her A levels. 'I didn't even know I was interested in the law', she says, 'until I started working in the local county court.'

## Legal beginnings

During her A level course at Littlehampton Community School, she had every intention of going to university to study drama and theatre studies. She obtained good grades in English literature, history and theatre studies, then decided to take a year out and earn some money to help finance her degree course. 'I worked in a supermarket for a year, and during that time I began to have second thoughts about university. It began to look very expensive – and acting isn't exactly a stable profession, so I started to look around for alternatives. I saw an advertisement for an administrative officer at Worthing County Court, sent in an application and got the job. It wasn't meant to be more than another temporary job while I worked out what I wanted to do, but as it turned out I loved the job. I enjoyed working with barristers, judges and solicitors and I found that I enjoyed learning about the law.' At first Lyndsey did general administrative work, but was soon promoted to the position of court clerk. 'This meant that I looked after the visiting judges and prepared papers for court hearings. I did most of my work, though, with the one resident judge. I sat with her in court and took notes, typed up her orders later and sent them to solicitors. Many cases involved repossessions from people who had defaulted on mortgage or rent payments, but I also saw custody proceedings in divorce cases. These could be very upsetting when you saw parents sitting at opposite ends of the court room.'

While employed at the court Lyndsey began to study for the examinations of the Institute of Legal Executives (ILEX) after seeing an advertisement from her local college, Northbrook, offering part-time courses.

## To legal advisory roles

Lyndsey was enjoying her job at the court but was beginning to feel limited. 'There was no possibility of ever giving any advice. I was not permitted to offer any opinion. I felt that I wanted a role where I could use my legal knowledge to help people by advising them. Through my ILEX studies I began to learn about other types of employment, and started to look at law firms.' So she found a job with a firm of solicitors in Brighton and worked there in the personal injuries department. She was recruited as an assistant to a partner and worked with her on complicated cases. Because of her relevant experience Lyndsey also had her own caseload of relatively straightforward cases.

After a year Lyndsey realised that although she had gained some useful experience, a law firm was not the right environment for her and decided to move into commercial work as an in-house lawyer. A local company that Lyndsey remembered from her court days advertised a position and she applied for it, without much hope, as she felt she was not sufficiently experienced. Luckily people at the firm remembered her too and she was offered the job.

## Litigation

Lyndsey's new job was with Credit Acceptance, a financial services firm that specialised in providing loans for car purchase. She was recruited to deal with complex legal cases involving debt recovery. 'They were not simple cases of default, but ones in which there was some dispute.' When necessary Lyndsey instructed barristers and accompanied them to court to take notes. She had by now finished the first part of her ILEX exams but had not begun part 2 (in which students begin to specialise in chosen aspects of law). She found her new job challenging – but once again found her previous experience helpful. After six months she was promoted and became head of the legal department! She now had 20 staff to manage – plus the person who had replaced her as litigation assistant. Some of her staff were older than she was. How did she feel about this? 'A little nervous at first as I was conscious of an age difference in some cases. But I realised that if people respected me and saw that I knew the work – and was fair – it should be alright. And it was, even though it was a steep learning curve. I took care to be a very hands-on manager and always did some of the day-to-day work myself.'

## Compliance

Lyndsey's next job was compliance manager, a role in which she worked closely with the managing director. (More information on compliance work is given in Sally Parker's profile, page 150.) Lyndsey enjoyed this job too and was pleased to have moved into business operations work. However, when Lyndsey had been with the company for four-and-a-half years the company was closed and all the staff made redundant. 'It was an American company and they had decided to pull out of the British market. But we did know that this was going to happen one year in advance.' Lyndsey was never actually unemployed. She was one of a handful of people kept on to help wind up the company – and while doing this learned about redundancy and employment law. She also managed to find another job and started work the day after leaving her old job.

The new job was in Richmond, Surrey. It was a small company and Lyndsey was employed to ensure that all aspects of its work complied with regulations set by the Financial Services Authority. She found that she enjoyed this work, but after one year decided to look for a similar job with a larger, more global company. This was when she moved to BUPA Insurance.

## Lyndsey's current job

'I now work in a small team with one other person in the compliance unit. We are advisers to the insurance business on its financial services legal/regulatory obligations. This involves researching and monitoring for developments and keeping the business abreast of such changes, and providing specific advice on internal processes and procedures to ensure the business operates in compliance with those legal and regulatory obligations. It includes reviewing documentation and providing advice on that, and meeting with, presenting to, and training colleagues in their understanding of their legal/regulatory obligations and how this is to be applied in practice in their day-to-day operations. It means striking a balance between regulation and business strategy and needs.

It is yet another challenging role. I have two hats. I need to understand what the numerous directives and all the regulations from the FSA mean. Sometimes it is like reading through an Act of Parliament, then interpreting it. The responsibility is mine. I have to make my own judgements. Next, I have to make sure that my colleagues in the business departments understand what this means to their work – and comply with it. I have to understand the business needs of the company too. Sometimes there is conflict. It is not that colleagues want to do anything wrong, but sometimes they see compliance requirements as restricting their possible options.

Although we are based in London, my colleague and I travel frequently to other offices in England to attend meetings or give presentations. We might pick topics ourselves – ones that we feel need explanation – or we might offer a refresher course. Sometimes we respond to a request for a presentation. I enjoy this side of my job, and I am always pleased when people tell me that I have explained complex legal documents to them in terms that they can understand.'

## Advice from Lyndsey

'I really would recommend the ILEX route. I wanted to continue with education but didn't want to stop work. By choosing to work and to study on a part-time basis, I was able to work and build a career alongside gaining the qualification. All my employers have supported me financially.'

## Career note

The minimum entry requirements are four GCSEs/S grades (A*-C/1-3) in academic subjects including English. However, many entrants have level 3 qualifications or degrees.

Trainee legal executives are also employed in local government legal departments of both district and county councils. Similar work is undertaken in some Civil Service departments, such as the Department for Constitutional Affairs (formerly the Lord Chancellor's Department), which administers the county courts, and the central criminal court. Police services, particularly the Metropolitan Police, have large prosecuting departments with their own legal staff.

Qualified legal executives may take a shortened training route to become solicitors.

In Scotland there is no exactly equivalent job and no single route to qualification. Staff are usually known as paralegals. Many employers train their staff completely on the job. Others expect them to attend a part-time paralegal studies course at Strathclyde University.

### Further information

**The Institute of Legal Executives** – Kempston Manor, Kempston, Bedford MK42 7AB. Tel: 01234 841000. www.ilexorg.uk

**Scottish Paralegal Association** – 26 Drumsheugh Gardens, Edinburgh EH3 7YR. www.scottish-paralegal.org.uk

## Related careers

Barrister's clerk

Licensed conveyancer

Legal secretary

Solicitor

---

# Gavin Watkins
## Trainee law costs draftsman – Thring Townsend Solicitors

When Gavin was doing his GCSEs, like many of his friends he assumed that he would probably go on to university. However, once he started his A levels, he realised that learning in the classroom really wasn't for him. He passed his IT, but didn't do so well in his other AS and A levels. Keen to find employment, but also to carry on learning, Gavin found a place on an Advanced Modern Apprenticeship (AMA) in accountancy (these are now known as Advanced Apprenticeships). The AMA involved being employed by an accountancy firm, training on the job and working towards qualifications through day or block release. He enjoyed this method of learning but, after a few months, realised that accountancy wasn't the right career.

Although Gavin knew that he wanted to work in an office, he wasn't sure exactly what to do. He decided to go to a local recruitment agency and found a job with Thring Townsend, a firm of solicitors in Bath, as a trainee legal assistant. He has been in the same firm ever since.

## Selection and induction

When Gavin first started at Thring Townsend, he spent the first day or so with the IT trainer learning how to use the computer system. A few weeks later, a formal induction was held. This comprised a range of activities and presentations from various members of staff in the firm. When Gavin applied for his current position as a trainee law costs draftsman (two years after starting in the firm), he had an internal interview. He also spent an afternoon secondment in the department. This not only gave Gavin the opportunity to find out whether the work suited him, but also allowed his manager to see whether he was the right person for the job.

## Training

Gavin's manager is an experienced costs draftsman so, at the moment, Gavin is learning on the job. However, soon he will be enrolling on a three-year course with the Association of Law Costs Draftsmen (ALCD) – probably with attendance once a month. Once qualified, Gavin will be able to call himself an Associate ALCD. Gavin's firm will pay for the course.

## Current role

Gavin has been in his current position for one year. Thring Townsend deals with two types of clients – those who are privately funded and others who are funded by legal aid (whereby the Government gives means-tested financial support to those who need help pursuing legal cases).

Solicitors are legally obliged to keep a log of everything that they do for each client, including how much time they spend on various activities – this might be interviews, phone calls, letters written, etc. All of this information is recorded using a computer package. Once a case is concluded, Gavin and his colleagues are given all this information. From this, Gavin makes up a 'bill of costs' and comes up with a total fee. For legal aid cases, this bill is sent to the Legal Services Commission so that the firm can recoup the costs of their services from public funds.

Accuracy is essential!

Gavin is really enjoying all aspects of his job. He particularly likes finding out about the details of various cases, but he recognises that confidentiality is vital.

## The future

At the moment, Gavin is not really sure where his career will progress. Although, once qualified, there is the option to go freelance, Gavin likes the security of working for a firm, so he will stay with Thring Townsend for the foreseeable future. In the long term, he would like to become a Fellow of the ALCD.

## Tips from Gavin

Even though Gavin had a false career start early on, he has now found something that challenges him. He has taken advantage of the training offered through his job and is open to ideas for the future. Gavin believes that it is important to find a style of learning that suits you – in his case learning at work seemed more appropriate to him than sitting in a classroom.

## Career note

Trainee law costs draftsmen must first find employment with a firm of solicitors, a government, local authority or other legal department or with a Fellow or Associate of the Association of Law Costs Draftsmen. They must then, within four years of becoming a student member, follow a course of study and take and pass the Association's examinations.

## Further information

**The Association of Law Costs Draftsmen** – Church Cottage, Church Lane, Stuston, Diss, Norfolk IP21 4AG. Tel: 01379 742702. www.alcd.org.uk

## Related careers

Accounting technician

Barrister's/advocate's clerk

Legal executive

Legal secretary

Licensed conveyancer

# Kieri White
## Fighter controller – Royal Air Force

Fighter control officers monitor the skies, working in a high-tech operations room on an RAF base or from aircraft. There are two types – weapons officers, who deal directly with the control of fighter aircraft, and systems officers, which is Kieri's specialism. Systems officers monitor wider air defence, using ground, sea and airborne systems.

## Background

Kieri always knew that she would join one of the uniformed services. Her parents were both in the Royal Navy, as were several relatives; she knew all about service life and was attracted to it. The question was – which one? 'I decided on the RAF after visiting the Armed Forces Careers Office. They sold it to me! I liked the sound of the jobs that would be open to me – and I didn't want to follow in my family's footsteps exactly. I did also apply to join the police but withdrew that application when the RAF accepted me.'

Kieri left her school, Ysgol Maes Garmon in Mold, Clwyd, three years ago with A levels in biology and English literature plus AS maths. She was, she says, under some pressure to apply to university but she knew that she didn't want this – 'I saw no point in doing a subject of no relevance to a career. I wanted to get a life and earn a living.' So, she stood her ground.

During the summer after leaving school Kieri worked for her father who now owns a landscape gardening business – to give herself some time to think about careers – and made her applications to the RAF and the police in the autumn.

## Selection

Selection for all three Armed Services is thorough. Candidates are chosen not merely on ability to do a particular job, but also on leadership potential as officers in charge of servicemen and women. Kieri had her first interview at the careers office and was recommended for the next stage.

This consisted of three days at RAF Cranwell in Lincolnshire, where she had a medical, took aptitude tests to find out which jobs she would be able to train for, and had two 45-minute in-depth interviews with two senior officers. She also took part in a series of group and individual leadership-potential and problem-solving exercises.

'One group exercise was a physical one in a hangar. We had to work out how to get a set of tyres from A to B, using ropes and avoiding obstacles. Another was a problem-solving one. We were given a scenario, which involved organising a jungle rescue with several possible means of transport and certain restrictions. For instance, going overland meant taking a route through mountains. We could only do that within certain hours. We had the use of a boat – but that was in a different location. We had to work out the best solution and then present it.' All the time the candidates were being observed and assessed on leadership, teamwork and communication skills. Kieri also had to do some similar exercises on her own and present her solutions to the selection panel. She also took part in a group discussion. 'This is always on a topic that you cannot prepare for. Ours was on ballet!'

About a month later Kieri heard that she had been accepted –and was required to pass a second medical specifically for the work of fighter control.

Why fighter control? 'Because I didn't want an admin job. I wanted to do something that would challenge me and that would change all the time. Flight crew was a possibility, but that didn't appeal either. One of the jobs that I had qualified for was fighter control, and I had discussed it in detail with one of the interviewing officers at Cranwell who did that job himself and told me a lot more about it.'

But before she could start training for fighter control Kieri first had to qualify as an officer. This meant six months of initial training – hard at first and for long hours with drill, kit maintenance, room inspections, weapons training. 'It was a shock at first but I quickly got used to it.'

Kieri was duly commissioned as a pilot officer and was posted as a 'holding officer' to RAF Leuchars in Scotland. 'Fighter-control courses begin at certain times of the year so while I was waiting for a place I gained experience in working with aircrew by arranging flying programmes. I did that for four months then went to RAF Boulmer in Northumberland to do the first stage of my professional training. This lasted four weeks. I did an air-defence foundation course and took more aptitude tests. As a result of these I was selected for surveillance work. (At this point you are streamed for surveillance or weapons – or some people return to Cranwell for selection for another job.)'

After a further eight months' training Kieri took up her first operational role on 'Quick Reaction Alert'. The work was in an underground bunker where controllers work shifts around the clock, 365 days a year. 'Our job is to assess threats from intruders into UK airspace – and alert a senior officer if we are not happy about particular movements. If necessary, a fighter plane can be sent up to intercept and escort the potential enemy plane out of our airspace. We don't just observe military aircraft, however. We receive the flight plans of every single plane, even civilian charter aircraft passing through our space. And we assist in any air emergencies, working with military and civilian controllers.'

Since training Kieri has worked as watch officer in the Falklands for four months, and has been seconded to the Royal Navy as part of an air liaison team in Sierra Leone. Here she lived onboard ship. She is now a deputy surveillance training officer at RAF Boulmer where she is responsible for 14 surveillance trainees. This job brings regular hours between Monday and Friday. Quite a change!

However, Kieri will be leaving this job in three weeks' time to begin training for flying duties. She will then become an air surveillance officer working on Sentry E-3D aircraft.

## Skills

What skills does she need for her work? 'Concentration – but also the ability to multitask. I have to be focused on the aircraft I am controlling in the air and at the same time be able to interact with colleagues in the weapons team. A sense of humour helps too. You can be very tired at 2am on the night shift. You need to be adaptable as well – although I have found that my body clock adjusts. When I am on shifts I work for two days and two nights – from 8 to 8 – and then have four days off.'

And what does she most enjoy? 'The variety, the challenge of new jobs – and the opportunity to travel both in the UK and abroad.'

## Being an officer

In addition to her specific job duties Kieri also has the non-technical responsibilities of all officers. She is currently responsible for the work of one sergeant, two corporals and ten airmen and women. She has to supervise their training, carry out their assessments and write reports, and deal with any issues regarding their work. But the role doesn't end there. Any one of her team could bring a personal problem to her at any time. What sort of problems? 'Anything from ones connected with work to a problem at home or concerning relationships. I try to advise – or know where to suggest they go for further help.' Is this difficult, especially as some of her team are older than she is? 'It seems a bit daunting at first but we are taught how to handle some personal issues during basic officer training. And there are further courses that you can go on if you wish.'

## Off duty

Kieri lives in the officers' mess where she has her own room and all her meals are provided. There is also a bar and a TV room. 'It's brilliant. I have lots of friends and it is rather like being at university – except that I am paid to be here!' There is a dress code, however. In the public rooms in the evenings 'smart casual' must be observed. For Kieri this means skirt or trousers but no jeans or trainers. Men need not wear a tie except on formal occasions. (This is the case in this particular mess; on some stations jeans are allowed.)

Social life in the services is always good. Kieri has plenty of opportunities to take part in sporting and other activities. She is captain of the station's volleyball team for instance. When she was posted away from home over Christmas (to the Falklands) parties were organised and entertainers came out from the UK to perform.

## Career note

To become an RAF officer you need five GCSEs/S grades at A\*-C/1-3, including English language and maths, plus two A levels/three Highers or equivalent in any subjects. You must also be a British citizen from birth or hold dual British and another nationality.

All RAF roles are open to women, with the sole exceptions of RAF Regiment officer and RAF Regiment gunner. The RAF Regiment carries out roles similar to front-line soldiers – and, as in the Army, women are still not recruited for roles that can involve fighting the enemy face to face. (The first woman fast-jet pilot qualified in 1991.)

## Further information

For further information contact your nearest:

**Armed Forces Careers Office** – Tel: 0845 605 5555.
www. af.mod.uk/careers

## Related careers

Air traffic controller (see the profile of Henry Marshall, page 217)

Police officer (see the profile of Heidi Schultz, page 155)

The Army

The Royal Navy and Royal Marines

# Chapter twelve

# Retail and marketing

## Sarah Gallimore
### Project assistant (business marketing) – Lloyds TSB

Sarah took A levels in business studies, English and history and an AS level in environmental science. She then went to university to study for a degree. Unfortunately, Sarah's health was in question and she found that she couldn't afford the time and money to continue with such a big commitment. She was unable to complete her degree and left university.

In order to earn some money and to gain valuable work experience, Sarah worked as a temp in various organisations. She eventually found herself working at the head office of Lloyds TSB. She was fortunate enough to be offered a full-time job within the business marketing department. There was no specific selection process, as she had already proved that she had competence in her role and the ability to take on a range of tasks.

## Induction

In order to help Sarah settle in, she was allocated a 'buddy'. This is a person, experienced in the organisation, who acts as a mentor, is able to show a new person around and is available in case of concerns or queries. Sarah also had meetings with her line manager and was given an induction pack with details of rules, regulations, job descriptions, useful phone numbers and organisation charts to show the structure of the business.

## Current role

The business marketing department is responsible for promoting Lloyds TSB services to all its business customers. This includes researching services and marketing these, for example, through direct mail. Sarah has now been working at Lloyds TSB for two-and-a-half years. In order to cope with her continuing health concerns, she works about 30 hours a week over three-and-a-half days. Within the marketing department, Sarah has a varied role. Each day she distributes the post and answers the telephone. She also deals with customers' problems and may divert callers to the relevant members of staff. She may also be involved in preparing presentations, organising meetings, diary keeping, minute taking at meetings, sorting out catering and arranging travel and hotels.

Sarah sometimes takes responsibility for certain aspects of project work with support from her line managers. She was recently involved with one particular piece of research looking at feedback from a pilot study where Lloyds TSB had introduced different levels of 'relationship' for its business customers. This involved briefing staff in an internal department who were conducting the research via an external company, attending all the meetings and having an input into the kinds of questions to be asked. Once all the results had been collected, Sarah analysed these and reported back to senior management on the research findings.

## Promotion

Sarah has recently been awarded promotion, which means that she will move up to the next staff grade. She will be involved at a more senior level in the type of work she currently carries out.

## Likes and dislikes

Sarah enjoys the variety in her job role. No two days are ever the same and she has been able to gain a good basic insight into many areas of the bank and into marketing in particular. On the negative side, being relatively new in the organisation, Sarah sometimes feels that she gets landed with some of the jobs that nobody else wants to do! However, she recognises that this is usually the same for all newcomers.

## The future

Sarah aims to reach a respectable level within her job and to earn a reasonable amount of money. She hopes to keep her work at a level she can cope with. Sarah would like to take every opportunity within the organisation to better herself and to gain qualifications, and has registered with the Open University to finish her degree and to make the most of her past study. Although her degree is not directly related to her job, she feels that it is well worth getting qualified.

## Tips from Sarah

'Remember that within many organisations there are lots of opportunities to take relevant courses and achieve qualifications. For instance, I have the chance to take the Chartered Institute of Marketing's Certificate because it is relevant to the work that I do. You need to have self-belief and confidence in your ability.'

## Career note

People employed in marketing can study for qualifications awarded either by the Chartered Institute of Marketing (CIM), which Sarah mentions, or the Communication, Advertising and Marketing Education Foundation (whose qualifications are now awarded by the CIM).

## Further information

**The Chartered Institute of Marketing** – Moor Hall, Cookham, Maidenhead, Berks SL6 9QH. Tel: 01628 427500. www.cim.co.uk

**The Communication, Advertising and Marketing Education Foundation** – Moor Hall, Cookham, Maidenhead SL6 9HQ. Tel: 01628 427120. www.camfoundation.com

## Related careers

Sales

Advertising

Market research

Public relations

# Kirk Armitt
## Management trainee – Arcadia Group plc

Kirk has A levels in business studies, geography and psychology, plus AS general studies, which he obtained at Hardenhuish School in Chippenham, Wiltshire. He was all set to apply for a business management degree until he looked into the cost. 'I decided it just wasn't financially viable.'

## Change of plan

Kirk previously had a weekend job in retailing with one of the major supermarket chains – and decided to look at the possibility of a retail management career. His manager encouraged him to apply for the company's management training programme but Kirk decided to look elsewhere. He started with an internet search and soon found details of the Arcadia scheme. He was so impressed that he went straight to the application page and began to complete the form. This took some time. 'I didn't realise how long it would take – several hours in fact. I knew that it was a popular programme and that I had to make a good impression, so I took my time over it. I took particular care when answering questions like, Give examples of your ability to work in a team, Have you ever been in a situation where you had to take charge? and Give an example of your ability to inspire and motivate other people. I had been chairman of young enterprise at school, treasurer of the school council and rugby captain, so I had some things to write about. When I had finished the form I checked it several times and I also asked my father to look at it.' A week after submitting the form Kirk was invited to an interview and assessment day in London.

## Selection

'I was so worried about being late that I got up at 4.30am to catch the first train. I was the first person to arrive! The day began with a meeting for all the applicants when we were told what would happen during the day. I then had an individual interview – with a manager from Dorothy Perkins and spent the rest of the day doing group tasks. I was so nervous during the interview that a pen I was fiddling with shot out of my hand and right across the room.'

The exercises focused on problem solving, strategic thinking, commercial understanding and also tested candidates' skills in working within a group. The activities were all related to the retail business. 'In one we were given the task to design an ideal shop-floor layout and we were observed throughout.'

Following the assessment day, Kirk was offered a place at the Burton store in Bath.

## First store

Kirk is on a 12-month management training programme with the Arcadia Group, which is one of the largest high-street fashion retailers in the UK with eight brands – Burton, Dorothy Perkins, Evans, Miss Selfridge, Outfit, Top Shop, Top Man and Wallis.

## Induction

The management trainees follow a 12-month training programme, which combines in-store development with a variety of structured activities. These include regular workshops, business assignments, placements in other Arcadia stores to help prepare for the first management appointment, and a personal development plan.

All trainees start on the same day and attend a national induction event held in London. They are introduced to the Group and given an overview by senior managers from the different brands, on their profiles and target customers. Presentations are also made by head-office personnel on functions such as buying, merchandising and distribution.

Before he started in Bath, Kirk spent time in Burton at Cribbs Causeway, near Bristol. This is an 'induction store' where the training manager covered cash handling, health and safety, and company practices.

## In-store training

Kirk is now more than halfway through his training programme and is doing very well. He has a programme folder, which specifies clear guidelines on the experience he should be gaining, the standards expected, and a timetable showing what he will be doing on different dates during the year. He says, 'When I first came here, the people on four-hour Saturday contracts knew more than I did! I'm still learning. In fact I think you never stop. Before Christmas I worked through the tasks in my folder and did all the basics. I have worked on the shop floor, in the stockroom and in the office and learned a lot about the things the customer doesn't see, like managing stock and staff. Since Christmas I have been concentrating more on back-of-house work and people management. I have a lot of responsibility in driving my own development and my manager is very supportive. We also receive support from other managers within the area, our brand training managers and area managers.

I also have to write reports and essays every two months. These are sent to my training manager in London and she assesses how fast I am learning.'

## Out-of-store training

Kirk will attend a number of workshops during the course, which cover topics like commercial management, leadership skills, management techniques, training styles and brand awareness. He is also working on a group project with other trainees to maximise the brand's potential in a commercial way. This will be presented to senior Arcadia personnel before the end of the programme.

A further part of his training sees him accompanying senior managers on store visits. 'I have 'branched' with my area manager who covers stores from Bath to Penzance – and visited stores with him. I have had every opportunity to show him what I am capable of. He always asks my opinion on assessment visits before he tells me his own. I have been on two visits with him so far, and am due to complete another three. I will also visit branch stores with the regional controller and possibly with the brand director.'

During the year Kirk will also work, for short periods, in two other stores taking on the responsibilities of the manager. The placements will be carefully selected by his own manager and area manager who will ensure that he gains a range of experience to prepare him for his first management appointment.

Has he made the right decision? 'Yes, very much so. Work is brilliant and I love it. Every day is different, and every day has its own challenges. I love everything about it and, of course, I am very interested in fashion. I enjoy being able to advise customers and give them the confidence to wear clothes that suit them.'

## Career progression

The management trainee programme is designed to lead to a first appointment as a deputy manager of a medium- to large-sized store or manager of a small store. From here, trainees can move into other stores and continue progression to a senior store manager. Trainees can also work towards an area manager role with responsibility for approximately 15-20 stores.

## Advice from Kirk

Kirk would advise anyone considering retail management to get a part-time job first and see whether they like the environment. It is very fast paced and continually changing. 'I would also advise getting some experience over the Christmas period. There is no other time like it. You can't believe it until you have experienced it for yourself.'

## Career note

Several department stores, chain stores and supermarkets recruit people with 18+ qualifications for retail management training schemes. Your personal/careers adviser will be able to tell you which ones you can approach. You are strongly advised to begin looking early as most schemes have a closing date in December or January. Competition for places is severe.

An alternative route into retail management is to work as a sales assistant and, after gaining experience, progress into management through an internal promotion scheme.

To join the Arcadia Group management training programme you would need five GCSEs/S grades at A*-C/1-3, including English and maths, plus either:

- two A levels
- four AS levels
- two Highers
- or a level 3 diploma from the Fashion Retail Academy.*

*The Fashion Retail Academy is a specialist college in central London, which is supported by major high-street retailers including the Arcadia Group, Argos, GUS, Marks & Spencer, Next and Tesco and by the London College of Fashion at the University of the Arts. Readers of this book are likely to be aiming for one of the other entry qualifications listed, but if you are interested you can obtain full details at www.fashionretailacademy.ac.uk

## Further information

Visit the website: www.arcadiagroup.co.uk/recruitment and click on 'school leavers'.

## Related careers

Buying

Marketing

Purchasing

Sales

# Gemma Wright
## Management trainee – Waitrose

Gemma, who has A levels in French, art and business studies, actually completed two years of a degree course in French and business studies before realising that she had made a mistake. 'It was a four-year course and I just couldn't face the thought of two more years.' The only job she knew anything about, she says, was retailing – through holiday jobs in a shoe shop and an independent department store. At this point Gemma was influenced by her mother, a former Waitrose training manager. She looked up the details of the management training scheme on the internet and emailed a request for an information pack. When she had read it she sent in a formal application and applied nowhere else.

## Selection

Gemma was called for a first interview with the assistant training manager for the South Central region – a group of stores that included ones in her home area. She was then invited to attend an assessment day in London with other applicants. Here she took part in several exercises, including role-play situations with different customers and a scenario where a group of applicants had to devise a strategy to promote excess stock –'to test our creativity'. There was also a formal interview with a branch manager.

The next stage was a second assessment day. The applicants had to give a flip-chart presentation on what they expected at work and their own objectives. Gemma was nervous but found that her study of French helped. She was used to verbal communication. Most of the day's activities were designed to test applicants' skills in working as a team. 'We did a treasure hunt in small groups while assessors observed to see how we interacted with one another. We also did a role play following a 'Richard and Judy' format and filmed ourselves doing it.'

Gemma successfully passed all the tests and started work in the store in Wokingham, an easy commute from home.

## In-store training

The first stage of the programme, which lasts two years, prepares trainees for a section manager position in one of the stores. Those who successfully complete this stage may then continue training for a further three years to become a department manager – a member of the senior branch-management team. Gemma had already visited the store and met her department manager. She also had a folder, which contained details of all the things she was expected to cover in her training. 'It was a huge folder with a timeline of my development and a list of tasks to be covered as I worked in each section. There was also space for me to record meetings and outcomes.' Gemma had coffee with her department manager and discussed what she would be doing. It was up to her to plan how to complete the tasks in the folder and to organise her time in different sections of the store. After this meeting she set off to introduce herself to staff and to arrange timings for work in each section.

She started in fruit and vegetables, where at first she shadowed the assistant manager and learned how to carry out routine tasks like ordering and stacking produce. There was more to the latter than she had realised. 'Stacking sounds simple, but there are a lot of rules to follow. I would have to check that the weight of items, their price tickets and the descriptions of countries of origin were all correct when putting out the produce.' A lot of lifting was involved but Gemma was taught how to do it correctly. Next came periods working in dry goods and fresh foods. These were very different sections. Dry goods involved Gemma in a lot more ordering work and in making sure that sufficient supplies were always in the warehouse. There was less stacking to do than in fruit and vegetables, as stock was not replaced as regularly. There was more paperwork since she had to write reports on the reasons for any price reductions. In fresh foods she learned how very quickly stock must be moved. 'A fine of £1,000 can be imposed for each out-of-date item. So if the section manager allows ten shepherd's pies to remain out after their expiry date the store could lose £10,000.' Gemma would normally have spent time in three other sections, patisserie, meat and fish. However, work there would have meant leaning forward to get items from the front of display counters. Gemma is only 5'1" (1m 55cm) and health and safety regulations meant that she should not risk injuring her back by leaning too far forwards.

During her time in Wokingham, Gemma was learning how to do every task she would later expect her staff to do. She also completed a project on the role of an assistant section manager, which she had to present to the branch manager, and attended several courses away from the branch in the company of other management trainees. 'These were excellent. We covered technical parts of the job, how to train staff, communication and presentation skills and even had assertiveness training.'

## Newbury

Gemma completed the first stage of training in just under one year and is now an assistant section manager in Newbury. How do staff members react to her being in this position at her age? 'I've been very lucky. Wokingham was a training branch so everyone was used to management trainees coming through. I was completely new to managing people and it was a steep learning curve, even though I enjoyed it. I think it is a question of attitude. I'm not domineering. I respect the staff and take an interest in them. You have to get to know your partners (the Waitrose term for staff members) really well so that you can weigh up which type of approach works and how individuals will react. I can leave some people to get on with things, while with others I have to state clearly exactly what I expect.'

## The future

Gemma aims to become a department manager as soon as possible. She will definitely stay with the company and counts herself lucky to have been accepted for the one job she wanted. She is also glad to have made an early start and says that had she finished her university course she would probably have made exactly the same career choice.

## Advice from Gemma

'To be a successful manager in retailing you need to have self-confidence. This will come as you develop, but it is important to have enough at the beginning to go round the store, introduce yourself to everyone and ask for their cooperation with your training plan.

You must be prepared to do work at times that is technically below your level. If you haven't got enough staff at some point and a shelf needs to be cleaned, you have to get on your hands and knees and do it.

You need a calm temperament – so that you do not become stressed when asked to do four different things at once!'

## Career note

Many department stores, chain stores and supermarkets recruit people with 18+ qualifications for retail management training schemes. Your Connexions/careers adviser will be able to tell you which ones you can approach. It is advisable to begin looking early as most schemes have a closing date in December or January. Competition for places is severe.

An alternative route into retail management is to work as a sales assistant and, after gaining experience, progress into management through an internal promotion scheme.

## Further information

You can email recruit@waitrose.co.uk or ring the staff and training department (Tel: 01344 824042) to request a brochure and an application form.

## Related careers

Buying

Marketing

Purchasing

Sales

# Chapter thirteen

# Scientific and technical

## Samantha Hubbard
### Process control engineer – UPM Shotton

Samantha (Sam) has always been passionate about knowing how and why things work. As a child she shared with her father, a builder by trade, a love of designing and building anything – from kit cars to remote-control airplanes. They even built a caravan from scratch. Design and technology was her favourite school subject and she designed and built a remote-control hovercraft for her GCSE project, using the technology she also used on her remote-control planes.

After A levels in design and technology and geography at Weatherhead High School, Wallasey, Cheshire, Sam did a one-year foundation course in engineering (a conversion course for would-be engineering degree students without A levels in appropriate subjects). She then enrolled on a degree course in design engineering at the University of Central Lancashire. BUT – 'The course was not right for me. There was too much 3-D and product design. I was interested in structures, pneumatics and mechanics etc. I wanted to take things apart and see how they worked. It was all too theoretical and with the wrong emphasis for what I wanted to do.'

So, Sam left after one term. By chance her mother spotted an advertisement from UPM Shotton, a paper mill manufacturing newsprint, in North Wales, which was recruiting Apprentices, and encouraged her to apply. After several interviews – 'They were very careful because I was older than the other applicants and also the only girl!' – Sam was accepted. Her first year was spent in off-the-job training – four days each week in a training centre and one at a college of further education. For the next three years she trained on the job and the day release to college continued. During the four-year Modern Apprenticeship Sam gained NVQ levels 1, 2 and 3 and a National Certificate in engineering plus a Higher National Certificate in measurement and control. But these were not enough for Sam! Her further achievements are impressive! She has an HND in engineering and management for which she studied at evening classes – and a BEng degree in computer and control engineering. For this Sam spent one day and evening each week at Liverpool John Moore's University. The company encouraged her and allowed her to take the day off each week, but she had to make up the time by starting work at 6am instead of 8am on the other four days! As if all this were not enough, she was pregnant with her second child when she sat her final exams, and her proudest moment, she says, was posing for her graduation photographs holding both children (aged one and two).

As an Apprentice and technician Sam enjoyed not knowing what she would be doing each day. 'The work was so diverse. One morning I could be programming the equipment that controls the paper machine and that afternoon changing a motor in excess of two tonnes, covered in grease, trying to get the machine up and running again.'

Working for all her qualifications demanded good time management. There was reading to be done outside timetabled classes and she also had assignments to complete. Sam does say, however, that doing these was much easier for her than for full-time students on the BEng course. 'I could do projects that were useful both to Shotton Paper and to my academic work. I could build something at work that tied in with what I was studying at university – and I enjoyed testing and integrating theory and practice. The full-timers had to do projects assigned by the university and these were much more theoretical. I could see why I was doing something and it made far more sense to me.'

Sam's time-management skills are necessary more than ever in her present job. She takes the boys to nursery every day – 'I am always the first to arrive and the last to collect'. Her elder son is very proud of her and talks about 'My mummy the engineer'. She is currently working towards registration as a Chartered Engineer.

## Sam's current responsibilities

Sam currently leads a small process-control department that serves the whole site. The team supports two paper machine lines – which means maintaining the quality control and distributive control systems, both of which are computerised, plus the process control equipment. 'It involves making sure that the machines work as efficiently as possible – by, for example, reducing the raw materials and energy used – while producing the best quality range. Our quality control systems mainly consist of a scanner at the paper machines measuring weight, moisture, thickness, colour and filler in the sheet, and we control these further back in the process using high-specification valves, hydraulic pressures of rolls, stock supply actuators, thermal heaters and chemical dosing. The distributive control systems are the programs that the operators use to run the machine, a graphics package that allows adjustments and to observe the measurements in the process, and the programming that controls these loops, motors and safety interlocks across the site.

The challenge of managing people is very exciting, as I had only wished to have a technical role previously but am enjoying all the intricacies of human resources, already finding that you learn about yourself as you coach others.'

Sam also conducts projects and has recently presented a paper on winder pulper consistency to the Institution of Engineering and Technology (IET) and given a presentation to retired IET members on UPM Shotton's 100% recycled-fibre process. 'One aspect of my work that I enjoy most is the challenge to make UPM Shotton's paper better than that of their competitors. I am constantly looking for new ways to save the company money and increase its attractiveness to the customer.'

## Promoting engineering

Sam is a role model for Women into Science and Engineering (WISE). In this capacity she visits schools and colleges to talk about engineering to mainly (but not always) female audiences. 'It is a very important role since we need more able young people to come into engineering. Sadly there is still a perception that engineers are grease monkeys in overalls. UPM Shotton is a Finnish company and when I visit Finland – or any other European country – I see how engineers are recognised as professionals on the same level as lawyers and accountants.'

## Advice from Sam

'There is such a breadth and range of career possibilities in engineering that whatever your particular interest there will be something to suit you. I personally enjoy getting my hands dirty but there are lots of jobs that involve computer, laboratory and desk work. Anyone can find their own career avenue.'

## Career note

Although many companies now prefer to recruit engineers who already hold degrees or HNDs, there are others that, like UPM Shotton, provide training for Apprentices and encourage them to qualify to degree level. Your personal/careers adviser will know which ones you can contact.

## Further information

**The Engineering Careers Information Service** – SEMTA House, 14 Upton Road, Watford, Herts WD18 OJT. Tel: 01923 238441. www.scienceworlds.co.uk/enginuity.cfm

**The Institution of Engineering and Technology** (formed from a merger of the former Institution of Electrical Engineers and the Institution of Incorporated Engineers) – Savoy Place, London WC2R OBL. Tel: 020 7240 1871. www.theiet.org/contacts/

**WISE** – 6th Floor, 10 Maltravers Street, London WC2R 3ER. Tel: 020 7557 6479. www.wisecampaign.org.uk

## Related careers

Other branches of engineering – e.g. aeronautical, chemical, marine, mechanical

# Tom Lengthorn
## Trainee technician – Thames Water

The training scheme Tom is following leads to work as a maintenance technician who keeps the machinery and equipment needed to treat water and sewage in full working order – pumps, gear boxes, engines, motors, and their electrical-control equipment. These technicians are based on a specific site, but travel throughout the Thames Water region as well as spending time in the workshops. Training is in electrical, electronic and mechanical engineering. The scheme includes cross-skilling to give an understanding of the different engineering disciplines. However, technicians choose to specialise in two of the disciplines – as either mechanical/electrical or electrical/electronic technicians. (They can cross-skill to the third discipline at a later date.)

Tom went from his comprehensive school to Bracknell College, to do a two-year, full-time National Diploma course in engineering. During his second year he decided that he would like to pursue a career in mechanical and electrical engineering and had a discussion with a careers adviser, who gave him details of several suitable companies. Tom made two applications, but as soon as he was offered a job by Thames Water he decided to accept it.

## Starting out

Tom joined the company's Advanced Apprenticeship programme in engineering maintenance, but because he had already qualified to level 3 standard he was put on an accelerated scheme. 'My first year was all spent at college on full salary. In fact it was spent at two colleges. On one day each week I went to Reading College to do a Higher National Certificate and I spent the other four at Kingston College of Further Education, learning machine skills like welding, bench fitting, machining using mills and lathes, and also electrical installation – I learned how to fit lighting circuits for example. These were all things that I had not studied in depth previously.'

In his second year Tom spent one day each week at college to complete his HNC and spent the other four days on site. At first he shadowed a senior technician, then progressed quite quickly to doing small parts of projects. 'When we were working on the biological filter beds, I helped to make new wheels for all the eight filter beds. (Each bed has 32 wheels.)

The new wheels were made from a more modern lightweight material to replace the old cast iron ones. I also made four of eight electrical control panels being built to replace some older ones. With each job I took on a little bit more responsibility. The best way to learn something is by doing it – and when others see that you can work safely, they let you do a lot for yourself. Then I moved on to working on projects by myself.

One project I enjoyed was designing a logic program for a programmable logic controller (PLC), which is the brain of the panel. Something I really enjoy about my job is the variety. I can move from mechanical to electrical work from one project to the next, and also work with complex computer systems.'

## Nearly qualified

Tom is now in the third and final year of his Apprenticeship and is concentrating on acquiring and providing evidence of all the skills he needs in order to complete the Apprenticeship. He has 13 workbooks, which contain the tasks he has to complete. 'I have *write-ups* to do for each job I have finished – 138 so far. For each one I have to reference the skills I have acquired and ask someone to sign it for me. I also have to do two *phase tests* for each skill and get marks for quality, accuracy and time.

Some of the skills could be difficult to claim because they are not ones that are covered here. So, I consult my training manager who arranges for me to be seconded to another company. I have spent a month with a motor company in Southampton to learn electrical motor skills, and I will have to go somewhere else to do some more work on hydraulic and pneumatic pipes. These are the sorts of things I discuss with the training manager during my regular assessments. It's a two-way process. Sometimes he says what he thinks I need to do next. Sometimes I ask for something. I am expected to take a lot of responsibility for my own learning.'

## Advice from Tom

'If you like doing practical things, and you like working outdoors a lot, this job is ideal. There is plenty of variety and within reason you can plan your own work. A supervisor puts tickets (giving details of different jobs) in my tray and I put them in order according to priority. Then, if I can, I do the outdoor jobs when the sun is shining and stay in the workshops in bad weather.

An HNC is hard work. My college day was from 9am to 6.30pm, and I had to spend most Sundays working at home on assignments. Apprentices must be prepared for some jokes and mickey taking! I can remember being given some stick – often for a couple of days if I had got something wrong with a job. The others don't let you forget it! It's all part of the system! I do it now with everyone else.'

## Career note

Thames Water is the largest water and waste water treatment company in the UK, supplying drinking water in London and the Thames Valley. It also removes and treats waste water. To become a trainee technician, following a four-year Advanced Apprenticeship, you would need at least four GCSEs at grades A*-C, including English and maths (the latter preferably at grade B or above), or to be studying for, or to have already obtained, a level 3 engineering qualification. A level applicants are also encouraged to apply for maintenance work. A level maths is useful. Applications should be made before February. Similar schemes are offered by other companies.

## Further information

**Thames Water** – Tel: 0845 166 3200. www.thameswater.co.uk

**The Engineering Careers Information Service** – SEMTA House, 14 Upton Road, Watford, Herts WD18 OJT. Tel: 01923 238441. www. scienceworlds.co.uk/enginuity.cfm

## Related careers

Other branches of engineering

# Greg Rogers
## Laboratory technician – Ciba Speciality Chemicals

Greg's career started almost by accident when personal circumstances forced a rethink part-way through an A level course. He had done well to GCSE level at Tytherington High School in Macclesfield, and was expecting to take the usual A level-to-university track, but financial considerations changed that and he found a laboratory job and worked towards relevant qualifications on a part-time basis. He certainly gives the impression of someone who is happy with the decisions he has made during his career so far. He now feels that he is progressing just as well as many of his school colleagues who followed the university track from school.

## Training

He applied for a post at Ciba, was delighted to get it, and found that his education options could take him just as far in science as his original plan might have done. He secured a training contract with day release to Stockport College to study for a Higher National Certificate (HNC). Passing each successive year of his HNC course gave him a pay rise every summer. Ciba supported his further education with course and exam fees and some study leave. He passed his HNC in chemistry which included topics such as computing, organic, inorganic and analytical chemistry, and practical training in writing logical project reports and making presentations of his findings. The reward for passing his HNC was that his training contract was replaced by a permanent staff contract and a further pay rise. He now has a variety of options if he wants to continue with higher education, including continuing part-time study at college towards a degree and beyond or specialist distance-learning courses leading to qualifications recognised by the British Coatings Federation.

The company also provides regular week-long courses to help staff keep abreast of the latest developments in the industry.

## Greg's work

Although the actual work differed from much of what he had been learning at college, Greg came to appreciate the grounding he got in basic lab techniques, and especially in accurate report writing. The company manufactures and sells pigments and dyes – that is colorants – which are used in plastics, inks and paints. So, if you are buying a can of Coke, a packet of Walker's crisps or a Mars bar, or a new ink cartridge for your computer printer, the chances are that the colour on the packaging or the colour in the ink cartridge was supplied to the ink manufacturer by Ciba Speciality Chemicals. It is quite possible that the colour on the cover of this book uses Ciba pigments.

The customers Greg's department supports, therefore, are manufacturers of all these products with their own technical and purchasing staff. This offers Greg variety, which he much appreciates. He is not undertaking original research into, for example, new types of pigment. He is looking at a huge range of applications of his company's pigment products on issues such as the precise mix of pigment to achieve the required colour, problems arising from particular mixes of pigment reacting together to produce unwanted manufacturing problems, and printing difficulties. Greg also has to keep abreast of the competition. So, if a rival company produces something new, the technical support team checks out the product to see how it differs from Ciba's products, and tips off the marketing department on their findings. For example, it could happen that a rival produces a pigment that it offers to a Ciba customer at a 10% discount. Greg could test the product and perhaps establish that the rival pigment is in fact weak, so the ink maker needs to use 10% more of the rival product than the Ciba pigment thus negating any cost savings.

## Day to day

The technical support department deals with any queries or complaints customers might bring forward. Typically a task will start with a phone call from a customer. Greg will usually take the query through from start to finish, working out which tests to use, undertaking the necessary programme of work, checking his findings with colleagues and producing a report. He could well have to present that report in person.

Customers know that Ciba's equipment is state of the art, and Greg might find himself helping a client solve a technical problem in designing a new product. Recently a customer complained that a pigment supplied by Ciba was not producing the desired effect. Greg was able to test his product and demonstrate that he was attempting to disperse the pigment more than recommended, thus causing it to break down and produce the wrong colour. Having discovered this, Greg produced a report and had to go to meet the customer at his factory to present his findings.

Greg uses some very recognisable lab equipment, such as accurate balances, which he used at college and even back at school. He also uses sophisticated specialist equipment such as a spectrophotometer working in conjunction with computers, and bead mills to test the dispersion properties of pigment. Another of his jobs was to assist a customer, who needed to produce something in 'Ferrari red', by taking a small photo spectrometer and laptop computer to a Ferrari dealer to measure the precise colour that Ciba was being asked to produce.

## Job satisfaction

Greg enjoys the variety. There is always something different coming in. He now feels he has a status in the company. For example, his department introduced the idea of product briefings for the telephone staff who receive incoming customer orders. This has gone down well and customers are receiving a better service as a result. When Greg was a trainee, he had a supervisor to ease him into the job. Now, he is the supervisor for new staff coming into the department.

He is not stuck in one lab every working day, but has the chance to travel to customers' establishments across the UK. There is also the chance to jet off to Switzerland on occasions to visit the Ciba head office there. He meets a wide range of people both at work and at meetings of his professional association, the Oil and Colour Chemists' Association, of which he is North West treasurer.

## Career note

Greg's lab work is in the field of chemical research. Relevant entry qualifications are A level maths and chemistry or Advanced Diplomas in science. Lab technicians work in a variety of other industries (for water companies and river authorities, the food industry, brewing) and other manufacturing industries (such as those for paper, polymers and metals).

Your choice will depend on where you live and your preference for either chemistry or biology.

Qualification routes for entry with level 3 qualifications in all labs will be similar to Greg's, although some employers would allow direct entry to a part-time degree course if the entry grades were good enough.

## Further information

**The Royal Society of Chemistry** – Burlington House, Piccadilly, London W1J OBA. Tel: 020 7437 8656. www.rsc.org

## Related careers

Laboratory work – biology/pharmacy

Medical laboratory technology

---

# Sarah Goodridge
## Dispensing Optician – Dollond & Aitchison

---

Sarah, who has A levels in maths, physics, English and general studies, trained as a dispensing optician with Dollond & Aitchison, but has now left that work to take up a position as business development manager for the company.

'I wanted to join the Royal Air Force', she says, 'but, ironically, was let down by my poor eyesight! What attracted me to this job was that I could train through a good training scheme for a hands-on job with people, that I would enjoy – and I'd have the option of moving over to the management side if I wished.'

Sarah had an initial screening interview with Dollond & Aitchison's regional manager in Worcester near her home. This was followed by a full day at an assessment centre that consisted of group tasks and one-to-one interviews. The group tasks were to assess how well she cooperated with other people. Another task – an individual one – was to test her ability to explain things in layman's language. 'I had to explain to one of the interviewers how to make one large shape from a selection of smaller ones, but I was not allowed to name them. I couldn't say 'I am going to use the triangle now', for instance, but had to describe its shape. This was testing my skill to explain things clearly without using technical terms or jargon. It is no good in dispensing optics to keep using terms like refractive index to customers!'

## The role

'An ophthalmic optician or optometrist is concerned with eye care; a dispensing optician with eye wear', says Sarah. 'When a customer leaves the ophthalmic optician after the eye test, they are handed over to the dispensing optician who goes through the prescription with them, makes sure that they understand it and works out which will be the best type of lens. We know through our training how light works, how lenses work and how the eye and lens interact. Light focuses on the back of the eye. Glasses change the way the light focuses by bending it. Customers depend on us to recommend glasses that will best meet their needs – and look attractive – so we have to get to know the customer and find out quite a lot about them. One of the aspects I enjoyed about the work was the interaction with people. We have to find out things like are the glasses to be for driving, reading, working at a computer or for constant use? Or are we talking about contact lenses? We get to know a lot about their lifestyle and hobbies. We might also help children to understand why they need glasses, or explain to an elderly person why they are unable to see as well as they used to.

Appearance is very important to people, so part of our job is to sell them the type of frames that best suit the shape of the face and the skin tone. I would never, for instance, recommend gold rims on a very light face, or round glasses on a round face. They accentuate the roundness whereas more angled ones look much better. We also have to establish whether people want simple, subtle or wacky frames. If the prescription is a simple one we would usually begin with the choice of frame, but if it is more complicated we would deal with the lens first. If someone is going to have bifocals or varifocals, for example, the lens has to do two or three jobs. It therefore has to be deeper and this might restrict the choice of frames.'

## Training

Sarah's training took three years and was a mixture of on-the-job training by colleagues and a correspondence course. At work she learned to work with customers, initially under supervision, to fit glasses and to deal with queries that arose after they had been purchased. The theory she studied covered physics, optics, anatomy and physiology, optical lenses, visual optics and fibre optics. She received regular reading material and question papers from the Association of British Dispensing Opticians (ABDO), and spent at least ten hours a week on study. There were 32 question papers to be answered each year. Sarah sent them off regularly and received written feedback from her tutor. She was commuting to work at the time and so did her reading on the train. Sunday afternoons were reserved for working on the question papers.

The training also included a four-week period of block release every year. This was a period of very intensive study, with a mix of 60% practical and 40% lectures. When Sarah trained this was done at City and Islington College and the company paid for Sarah to stay in London. Now, courses are run at ABDO's own college in Kent.

Each year there was a written exam to take, and in the final year a practical one in which she had to fit and adjust frames plus an oral. In this she had to tell the examiners how she would dispense prescriptions she had just been given and explain how she would solve certain problems customers might have.

She was given a lot of support while doing the course. A tutor was always available by phone and Dollond & Aitchison had its own tutors who could also be contacted. Dollond & Aitchison were also very helpful in setting mock exams for their trainees.

## Promotion

As soon as she qualified, Sarah moved to Hinckley to manage a branch of Dollond & Aitchison and from there moved to Derby to manage a larger branch where she had 15 staff. This is a typical route she says. Most of Dollond & Aitchison's dispensing opticians become managers soon after qualifying and have a promotion path open to them in regional management or head-office work. Some, however, prefer to move on to training for contact lens fitting, which requires a further course.

The route Sarah chose has taken her to the Birmingham head office where she is developing work with national companies. Employers of people who use computers for more than one hour a day must pay for them to have eye tests and, if necessary, pay for glasses. Sarah is developing a scheme under which Dollond & Aitchison will provide a sight test and eyewear scheme for companies, through its branch network.

She no longer works in dispensing, but she is an ABDO tutor and marks trainees' papers. 'It is difficult to find enough people who are willing to train and become tutors. I am grateful that someone did it for me so that I could qualify. I see it as a way of putting something back.'

## Rewards

Sarah found work as a dispensing optician very rewarding. 'We can make a real difference. It's a wonderful feeling when someone tells you that you have made them look ten years younger or when you help a child to accept wearing glasses by guiding them to the right frames.'

## Sarah's advice

'You must be prepared to accept responsibility. People trust opticians with one of their most precious possessions – their sight. It is very useful before training to have some background in working with the public, perhaps in a part-time job. While training you have to be very organised and set aside regular times for studying. I set myself a work plan and stuck to it.'

## Career note

To train as a dispensing optician, you would need a minimum of grade B in GCSE or equivalent in maths plus four more GCSEs/equivalent at grades A*-C, which must include English literature or language and a science-based subject.

It is also possible to train through a two-year full-time course and follow this with a salaried pre-registration year, under the supervision of a qualified optician, or through a full-time degree course that leads to the ABDO Fellowship Diploma and a BSc honours degree in optical management, dispensing optics or ophthalmic dispensing. A further possibility for trainees who live near Bradford, Cambridge, Glasgow or London is to follow a day-release course rather than study through distance learning.

There are good opportunities for registered dispensing opticians in the UK. Most work in private practice, with a few working in hospitals or teaching.

### Further information

**Association of British Dispensing Opticians** – 199 Gloucester Terrace, London W2 6LD. Tel: 020 7298 5100. www.abdo.org.uk

### Related careers

Optometry (ophthalmic optician)

Orthoptics

Medical physics

# Lee Irwin
## Data field engineer (Apprentice) – British Telecom

Prior to finding a full-time job, Lee took an Advanced GNVQ (now applied A level) in business at his school's sixth form. Although Lee attended various open days at universities and was offered a place at the University of the West of England, he was not 100% sure that this was what he wanted to do.

An Advanced Apprenticeship scheme at British Telecom (BT) was advertised in national newspapers, including the *Daily Mirror*, which is where Lee spotted it. He was keen to undertake a programme offering both off- and on-the-job training as he felt that this could lead to a promising career. As Lee's father works for BT, he was already familiar with some of the benefits of working for the company.

### Selection and induction

GCSE grades A*-C were requested in maths, English and science. Lee completed the necessary application forms and was then called to a formal interview. He was pleased when he was offered a contract of employment (subject to a medical and proof of his grades). Lee attended a national induction day where all newly-employed Apprentices from the Midlands, Wales and the West came together. They were formally introduced to the company and carried out various team-building exercises. Following this he attended a composite safety course, and since then he has been on local job-related training events.

### Training

Training is compulsory on an Apprenticeship programme. Lee is in the process of being assessed for the NVQ level 2 and 3 in telecommunications. He has successfully completed the BTEC National Certificate in electronics with distinctions, and is currently completing the first year of the Higher National Certificate. Lee has also completed his key skills at level 3.

Part of Lee's training involved carrying out a project of his choice. He investigated health and safety within BT and identified the common causes of accidents. Lee presented his findings and put forward recommendations at a presentation to managers within the company. They were so impressed with Lee's contributions that he was given the award of Apprentice of the Year.

## The work

Lee works a standard working week. At the moment he is unable to do overtime because he is still on the Apprenticeship scheme.

He works in the data field division of BT, where they provide data and voice circuits for large or small business customers. A typical day includes providing a circuit from his exchange to the customer's premises, fitting the appropriate network equipment and testing the circuit before handing it over to the customer to use. Lee may also spend time maintaining or recovering data and voice circuits and related equipment.

Lee likes the physical, hands-on aspects of the job. He has many benefits, including a van, a laptop computer with internet access, discounts on BT products and services and a pension scheme, as well as a well-paid job.

## Aspirations

Lee has now worked for BT for two years and seven months. His Apprenticeship period lasts for three years. Lee hopes to achieve promotion to a higher grade engineer within the first year after his Apprenticeship. He hopes that his HNC will help him achieve promotion to managerial level in the future. In the meantime, he recognises that he has to continue to gain experience of the technical side of engineering.

## Tips from Lee

'When applying for an Apprenticeship, although it isn't compulsory, I'm sure it helps if you are able to show that you are up for further education – my Advanced GNVQ certainly prepared me well for the programme. You also need to be able to work as a member of a team as well as on your own, to think logically and be able to solve problems. Although I have pointed out the many advantages of an Apprenticeship, you must bear in mind that it is demanding. I sometimes find training and working at the same time extremely challenging.'

## Career note

For further information on Apprenticeships see Chapter five.

## Further information

**British Telecom** – www.btplc.com/Careercentre

**The Engineering Careers Information Service** – SEMTA House, 14 Upton Road, Watford, Herts WD18 OJT. Tel: 01923 238441. www.scienceworlds.co.uk/enginuity.cfm

## Related careers

Other branches of engineering

# Chapter fourteen

# Construction, surveying and property

## Tom Winter
### Trainee design coordinator – Willmott Dixon

Tom works for Willmott Dixon (a major construction company) and is currently in his fourth and final year of the company's non-graduate management training scheme.

When Tom was thinking about his career choices during his GCSE year, he realised that the construction industry would suit him. He went on to take an Advanced GNVQ (now applied A level) in construction and the built environment. As he had already decided that construction was for him, he felt that this course would be more relevant than A levels.

## Selection and induction

There was fierce competition to get a job with Willmott Dixon as the company has a reputation within the construction industry for providing good training schemes.

On starting in the company, Tom attended Willmott Dixon's set induction training programme. This included finding out about the company and its facilities, communication processes, policies, procedures and conditions of employment. It also covered health and safety, job roles, etc. After the induction period, Tom went on various other introductory-level courses, e.g. in health and safety, first aid, IT and team building.

## Job role

Tom is training to be a design coordinator. This is an interesting and varied job. He goes on site, talks to consultants, reviews drawings in the office (e.g. to solve problems with designs) and attends meetings. He feels that his job gives him a good balance between theory and practical work.

In order to do his job effectively, Tom says that the main skills he needs are the ability to communicate with people at all levels, enthusiasm, a willingness to adapt to new situations and time management. The latter has been a challenge, but Tom feels that he has really improved the way in which he organises his work and study.

## On- and off-the-job training

Tom works four days a week and goes to university one day a week. Willmott Dixon's training scheme involves going on secondments to various internal departments. This has given Tom an awareness of the workings of the company, an understanding of careers within the industry, an appreciation of how his own role influences and impacts on others, and a wider understanding of his own job. Because Tom is experiencing the work of a variety of departments, there is always the possibility to change disciplines if he wants to in the future.

In addition, Tom has attended some CITB trade-awareness courses. This has helped him understand who does what on site, so that as a manager he doesn't expect craftspeople to do unreasonable tasks. As part of Tom's training scheme, he is taking a BSc in construction management at the University of Westminster. This is through day release over five years. He realises that he could have gone to university on a full-time course, but his older sister had found the cost of full-time university study a strain. He felt that getting a job with training and going to university part time would be better for him – he now gets a good salary, a company car and the added bonus that Willmott Dixon pays his university fees! Even more importantly, Tom is finding that his university course is giving him an insight into the industry and he is able to see the theory from his course put into practice at work.

Tom finds that it's good fun to be a student for one day a week – he gets to wear what he wants and enjoys the relaxed atmosphere. However, he says that studying by day release can be tough – you work for four full days, have one day at university and then have to spend time studying at home. You have to be very determined to get your work out in the evenings when an assignment has to be completed.

## The future

Tom knows that his work is appreciated and he feels that he has developed confidence in doing his job role. Although the work can be tough, he is really enjoying learning while working.

Performance permitting, at the end of the training scheme, Tom will be promoted to assistant design coordinator. He will finish his degree and complete his dissertation and then start an in-house management development scheme. By the time Tom completes his initial training, he will be well qualified and should have a good position within the industry and the team at Willmott Dixon.

Training doesn't stop there – Tom recognises that he will continue learning throughout his working life. However, at some point, he'd like to fit in some time to travel.

## Tips from Tom

Some of Tom's friends are taking the same degree on a full-time basis. But doing a course part time gives you the added benefit of support and back up from work and the ability to see the practical application of your studies. Tom has noticed a huge difference between students studying full time and those taking his course part time. He knows that when his friends finish their full-time degree, they will then have to find jobs and start training from scratch.

Finally, Tom says that if you are looking for work-based training rather than a full-time course, it's very important to find an organisation with a sound track record in training their staff.

## Career note

Other construction firms may be willing to accept you on a management training scheme, although sometimes these are aimed at graduates. If you are interested in this type of work, you should write to local construction companies or look on their websites to investigate whether or not they have suitable training opportunities. Individual employers will set their own entry requirements for their training schemes. Another way to train with an employer is to take an Advanced Apprenticeship in construction. Apprenticeships involve training in the workplace and you would work towards at least NVQ level 3, a technical certificate (such as a BTEC National or City and Guilds qualification) and key skills. The industry's Construction Apprenticeship Scheme (CAS) also offers training with an employer, leading to NVQs.

Your local Connexions/careers service or ConstructionSkills office can help you find opportunities through work-based learning.

## Further information

**ConstructionSkills** – to find out the address and phone number of your local office Tel: 01485 577 577. Alternatively, you can access the contact details of your local office through www.citb-constructionskills.co.uk/training

For further information about careers, qualifications and Apprenticeships in the construction industry, see www.bconstructive.co.uk

## Related careers

Architecture

Civil and structural engineering

Surveying

---

# Phillip Mann
## Property sales manager – Fox and Sons

---

Estate agency was not Phillip's first choice of career. However, he loves his job – proof that you can be successful if you have to change direction! Originally he was interested in art and design and began an A level course in art, graphic communication and media studies. Work didn't go well though – and Phillip left to take up an Advanced Apprenticeship in IT with the Hampshire Constabulary in Winchester. He completed the Apprenticeship, gained an NVQ level 3 in IT and stayed with the police for two years. Then, his interest in design resurfaced and he decided to return to college full time – this time on a National Diploma in graphic design at Basingstoke College of Technology. He loved it, but 'When I finished the course I wrote to every graphic design studio in Southern England. I got lots of kind replies but no job offers.'

### New choices

Phillip became interested in some kind of sales role. A friend owned an estate agency and appeared to be doing very well, so Phillip discussed the work with him, then made some job applications. He was successful and started work with a leading estate agent in Southampton. It was, he says, an excellent office to begin in – one of the largest in the

South. He gained some good experience, during the week did mainly viewings (accompanying prospective purchasers to look at houses) and at weekends worked in the office. He was ambitious and asked to make visits with valuers to learn about their job.

## Career progression

After a year Phillip decided to move on. He went to another firm of estate agents, in Eastleigh, between Southampton and Winchester. 'I received excellent induction training there. I was regarded as a trainee for three months and learned all about the legislation involved in buying and selling properties.' Then, after a year he moved to Romsey to work for Fox and Sons, a large chain with over 320 offices countrywide.

Here, Phillip got his big break. After a month's in-depth training he started valuing. He had a 'brilliant teacher, William, who had worked in estate agency for 15 years.' Nine months later William was promoted to manage the Southampton branch and Phillip was offered the role of day-to-day manager of the Romsey office, reporting to William. After nearly two years in Romsey, Phillip moved to the Winchester branch of Fox and Sons. It is a large branch with eight full-time staff, two part time and two more who work at weekends – this includes valuers, sales negotiators, administrators and a financial services adviser. Phillip is the property sales manager – and main valuer in the office.

## Phillip's role

'Clients come to us through recommendation or after seeing our advertisements in local press. Many invite more than one agent to visit, so I have to try to win the business for Fox and Sons. I allow about an hour for an initial visit. Assessing the value of a property is only a very small part of my job role. The majority of the time I invest with potential clients is spent building a rapport with them, and explaining our services and how we can best help them to sell their most important and valuable asset. I also have to encourage them to accept a realistic price. Obviously I want to make as much money for them as I can, but it's impossible to sell at an inflated price. These days, though, thanks to the interest in property prices, most people are already aware of approximately how much their house is worth. I show them details of prices we have achieved for similar properties, give them a value and quote a fee. I then keep in touch by phone over the next few weeks.

If I get the instruction I allow an hour and a half for the second visit. I find out what sort of publicity the vendor wants. This can range from low-key marketing, without much advertising, to the full works, with a board outside, newspaper and internet advertising with virtual tours. Clients vary. Some really do want to restrict the numbers of people visiting their home; others want to progress quickly and want all the services. I have to take room and garden measurements – and complete a lot of paperwork during the visit. Estate agency has become much more regulated and the vendor has to disclose a lot of detail about the property – including now any issues with neighbours.

I try to do no more than four visits a day because I have to do follow-up paperwork – and at more than that number I wouldn't feel that I was giving clients good value.

Back in the office, within 24 hours, I write a marketing report detailing the services we will provide and send that to the vendor. Next, I draw up a description and floor plan and send it back to the vendor who signs that it is accurate. I have to double check that the details are accurate and that I haven't missed anything. (For example I can't put 'fully double-glazed' only to find later that the vendor forgot about one small, single-glazed window!)

Then I have follow-up work to do. I might have discovered that a vendor also wants to look at properties, so I pass the details to our sales team. Or they might want a quote for conveyancing or advice from our financial adviser on obtaining a mortgage. I pass all this information on to appropriate colleagues. This is very important as, in addition to basic salaries, we receive monthly commissions depending on how well the branch has done. (I know that in some agencies staff get individual commission but we work as a team.)'

## What Phillip enjoys

- 'Most of all I like the variety. I meet so many different people.

- There are incentives if you do well. I've had a day at the races for instance.

- I really like getting return business. When someone comes back a few years later and asks for you by name to sell their next house, you know that you must have done well the first time.

- On the personal front I have become more confident. I can speak to people easily and I know that I could do any job in customer service.'

## Advice from Phillip

- 'Be prepared to move, even if only locally, in order to get a breadth of experience.

- Expect long hours! Officially I work from 8.30am to 6pm, but I am always in the office at 8.15am and some days I don't get away until 8pm. The early evening is a good time to make contact phone calls – and some people can only arrange viewing visits after they have finished work.'

## Career note

There are no minimum qualifications required to become an estate agent, but professional qualifications are available. Many employers would expect you to study for one of them. Phillip has received in-house training so far, but might decide to do the National Association of Estate Agents (NAEA) qualification later on.

The NAEA in partnership with TTC Training offers NVQs in residential estate agency and an examination-based Technical Award in Sale of Residential Property. There are no minimum entry requirements.

Some estate agents have qualified as surveyors through the Royal Institute of Chartered Surveyors (RICS). It is possible to gain its qualification by studying part time or through distance learning for a degree or diploma in surveying, which has a general practice specialism. The minimum qualifications required are five GCSEs/S grades at A*-C/1-3, including English and maths, and two A levels/three Highers.

## Further information

**The National Association of Estate Agents** – Arbon House, 21 Jury Street, Warwick CV34 4EH. Tel: 01926 496800. www.naea.co.uk

**The Royal Institution of Chartered Surveyors** – Surveyor Court, Westwood Way, Coventry CV4 8JE. Tel: 0870 333 1600. www.rics.org

## Related careers

Auctioneering and valuing

Sales

Surveying

# Matthew Morfoot
## Trainee quantity surveyor – Hambleton Steel

Hambleton Steel is a structural steelwork designer and fabricator, based in North Yorkshire. The company provides steelwork for all types of construction, including commercial offices, educational, industrial, residential and retail premises, warehouses, and sport and leisure complexes. Its project teams work throughout a whole contract process, from estimates through design, fabrication and erection. Matthew has worked for the company since leaving Queen Elizabeth Sixth Form College, Darlington, in 2006 with A levels in economics, history, sociology and general studies.

## Career decisions and advice

Matthew always knew that he did not want full-time higher education. What he did know was that he wanted to train and gain a professional qualification in employment. The question was – in which career area? He knew that he was not interested in retailing, having worked part time in a supermarket – but other than that he had no clear ideas. Was there any pressure to apply for a full-time degree course? 'Some, yes. It seemed to be the first path all my teachers thought of – and almost everyone else was filling in UCAS forms. But when I made it clear that this was not what I wanted, it wasn't a problem and they accepted it.'

Matthew requested several interviews with his college careers advisers, who he found very helpful. They explored several career areas – and it was when Matthew mentioned that he would not mind being office based, but would not like to be there all day, that one of them suggested the construction industry. 'She said that I would be expected to attend meetings with clients and make some site visits.'

Matthew read about the industry and researched the different jobs, using his college careers library, and in particular the learndirect website (www. learndirect.co.uk). Eventually, he hit on quantity surveying. 'A lot of people have the wrong idea about quantity surveying. They think that it is about measuring sites or counting bricks, but in fact it is more financial. It is probably quite similar to some types of accountancy – but in a technical industry.' (For a definition of quantity surveying see page 46.)

## Application

Matthew now had a stroke of luck. He had been advised that he should start to write letters to possible employers or look for job advertisements by the late spring or early summer. Before he had begun to do so, however, Hambleton Steel contacted Queen Elizabeth's careers department to say that they were looking for a trainee. Matthew applied, was interviewed and accepted.

Matthew went for an interview, which was really more of an informal discussion. It was with the company's commercial manager, Matthew's present boss who is responsible for his training. 'He asked me what I knew about the construction industry and why I had chosen quantity surveying in particular. I had my answers ready and they seemed to go down quite well. He also asked me why I had chosen this training route, and he was pleased when I said that I had thought it out very carefully and that the full-time degree route had no appeal for me at all. I realised that he wanted to find someone whom he would enjoy working with and training – and luckily, I seemed to fit. He also asked whether I could drive, as it would be necessary when going out to meetings. I was already learning so I had to make sure I passed my test as soon as I could. I also had to take out a bank loan to buy a car. Fortunately, I am still living at home so my living expenses are not too high.'

## Matthew's training

Matthew shares an office with his boss and learns from him all the time. 'It's rather like the master and apprentice relationship, except that I am not on an Apprenticeship programme. I observe everything that he does and learn from him. He is a very good teacher and even when he is really busy he always finds time to explain things. I go with him to all his meetings and learn all the time from these too.

I go to pre-start meetings, for instance. When Hambleton has won a contract – perhaps to build a factory – there has to be a meeting between our contracts manager, the client's contracts manager, architects and engineers. We go too and discuss the way the building is to be constructed, health and safety regulations, and how all the monthly payments are to be made. We have to be sure that we are all speaking the same language. I have also been out to visit some sites to see what is going on and also to discuss *variations*. If the client wants any changes to the original specifications – say two additional beams – quantity surveyors go to assess the cost. I have also been on a visit to Guernsey with the company land surveyor.'

## University

Matthew is attending university – on one day each week, with his tuition fees paid by his employer. He is enrolled on a BSc degree course in quantity surveying at Leeds Metropolitan University, which he attends every Monday. It is a long day. Lectures are from 9am to 5pm with just one hour for lunch. On top of that, Matthew has a two-hour train journey.

Matthew has just finished the first semester. 'It was very much a foundation course to bring us all up to the same level and to give us an introduction to the construction industry. We covered topics like CAD (computer assisted design), IT, introduction to construction technology and all the elements involved in building a house. The second semester has just started and I have modules in environmental science and services, land surveying and general surveying. Quantity surveying and estimating will come later.'

In addition to his work at university every Monday, Matthew has to do around four hours' private study each week. He sets aside time on Sunday afternoons for this.

Is the study very technical? 'No. The surveying modules do require some basic knowledge of maths and physics, but certainly not to A level standard. I have double science at GCSE rather than single subject physics, but I have been told that this is sufficient.'

Is Matthew still sure that he has made the right decision? 'Yes, definitely. I enjoy everything about my work, and learning on the job with what I am learning backed up by academic study one day a week is exactly the right route for me. Plus I am earning a salary and I will not have any student debts to pay off.'

## The future

Matthew expects to stay with Hambleton Steel when he is qualified. 'They won't expect me to leave after spending all this money training me! I'm really being trained to be the present surveyor's successor. In fact, one or two people here joke and call me the 'heir apparent.'

## Matthew's advice

'If you know that this method of training is what you want, you must work at finding out first what you want to do and then to organise a job-hunt. You shouldn't sit back while other students do their UCAS form and go for interviews. You can get all the advice in the world but you have to find the job. It is up to you to research careers and companies while they are researching universities. And you will probably have to write a lot of letters or fill in application forms. I was very lucky indeed. Not many people get the first job they apply for!'

## Career note

Most surveyors aim for the full professional qualification of the Royal Institution of Chartered Surveyors (RICS). After completing an approved degree or diploma, which forms the academic stage, either through a full-time course or a part-time one as Matthew is doing, they then complete the professional stage while in employment.

## Further information

**The Royal Institution of Chartered Surveyors** – Surveyor Court, Westwood Way, Coventry CV4 8JE. Tel: 0870 333 1600. www.rics.org

## Related careers

Building surveying

Building control

Civil and structural engineering

Construction management

General practice surveying

# Jake Wilks
## CAD technician – Barton Willmore

Jake works in the Reading offices of Barton Willmore – a consultancy that offers a comprehensive planning and design service throughout the UK, identifying sites for development; conducting land studies; site and sustainability appraisals; urban regeneration; urban design/townscape studies; minerals, waste and energy planning. On the building side, the firm is involved in residential and commercial developments, retail developments and leisure facilities. In total, it employs more than 200 town planners, architects and environmental consultants. Jake is based in the housing department.

Jake says that teachers at his school in Reading did not push him towards full-time higher education, because they could see that his heart wasn't in it. 'I didn't like doing A levels very much, even though I had chosen my best subjects.' Despite that, he achieved very creditable passes in A level design and technology and business studies with an AS in maths.

## Career decisions

Jake saw no point in going to university without a subject or career in mind. He still did not know what he wanted to do though – other than that design was his favourite subject. It was a friend's mother, a careers adviser, who told him about a vacancy at Barton Willmore and suggested that he apply for it. He sent in his CV (which had been prepared in school during careers lessons) and was invited for interview. 'It was quite formal with two people, one from human resources and one from the technical side, who is now my boss. They asked me a lot of detailed questions, but they were all relevant to the job and my interest in it, rather than about my outside interests. They showed me some of the work that they produced and then took me on a tour.' This was on a Tuesday. Jake was offered the job two days later because the firm wanted him to be able to enrol on a day-release course leading to a National Diploma in building studies the following week.

## Jake's role

Jake does different kinds of CAD work. 'Sometimes I'm working on standard house types – doing the drawings of both the inside and outside of the building. At other times I could be working on site plans. This means drawing the whole development scheme, with the houses laid out on the site. I also do working drawings that set out the dimensions of the houses and show where the services and windows will be, and conveyancing plans. These are for all the legal work connected with designing a development and show all the legal boundaries, such as the land owned by each individual house or flat, and the allocated parking spaces.'

Where does his work come from? 'Some of it is given to me directly by my boss and some comes from senior technicians who need some assistance. I have to organise my own workload and if too many people ask me to do things at the same time I have to discuss with them which really has to take priority. I know now how to estimate how long certain jobs will take and can say when I expect to be free. On any one day I might do several small jobs or I might spend the whole day on one project. I did a site plan recently, for instance, that took three weeks – working on it every day. At the moment all my work is checked, but as I get more experienced I will take over responsibility for my work.'

## College

This is hard work, Jake says. In fact he doesn't know how some of the other students, with homes and families, manage to get the work done. He is lucky as he still lives at home. He is now in his second year and the college day is from 9am until 8pm – 'It's a big course condensed into one day a week' – and he has to do at least the equivalent of an additional day's study in his own time.

## The future

When he has finished the National Diploma, Jake will start on an HND course. He intends to work his way up in the company and become a senior technician or an architectural technologist. He could even take a degree if he wished, but has no plans to do so as yet.

## Jake's advice

'Think carefully, make your decision and don't be influenced by anyone else. I know that I wouldn't have liked university. I couldn't wait to get to work. I'm much better suited to working my way up in a job.'

## Career note

A Higher National Certificate or Diploma in building studies can lead to a wide range of careers in surveying and property. See the other careers in this chapter for ideas.

## Further information

**Chartered Institute of Building** – Englemere, Kings Ride, Ascot, Berkshire SL5 7TB. Tel: 01344 630700. www.ciob.org.uk

**The Royal Town Planning Institute** – 41 Botolph Lane, London EC3R 8DL. Tel: 020 7929 9494. www.rtpi.org.uk

## Related careers

Architecture

Building control

Building management

Planning and development surveying

Quantity surveying

Town planning

# Chapter fifteen

# Transport, travel and logistics

## Gemma Lawson
### A varied career

Gemma, who is currently working for the David Lloyd Organisation in Teesside, has had a varied career in tourism, travel and leisure.

### First job

When Gemma left Queen Elizabeth Sixth Form College in Darlington with an Advanced GNVQ in leisure and tourism (now an applied A level) she went to the University of Lincoln to do a degree in tourism. Unfortunately, after two years, she had to leave for personal reasons and went back home to take up a temporary job as a membership adviser with the health-club chain Bannatyne Fitness Ltd where she showed prospective members around and encouraged them to join. She did well there – and stayed to make a career. She was then promoted to the job of sales and marketing manager for a new club that was being built, which meant a move to Kent. 'I had to encourage people to join a club that wasn't even built – working from a portakabin and showing them illustrations.' She was good at this and met her target of enrolling 2,000 members.

### Into tourism

Gemma then decided that she would like to get into the travel business and applied to Thomson Holidays to become a resort representative. First of all she had a telephone interview, then having passed that was invited to an interview day where she had to give a prepared presentation on her favourite holiday destination – 'this was to see how well I could sell' – and had an individual interview. The interviewer concentrated on finding out about Gemma's customer-service and problem-solving skills, together with her degree of maturity and independence. 'I had to convince them that I would be all right living overseas without having my parents around.' She was offered a job there and then, and a few weeks later began a one-week training course.

The trainees learned about customer service, health and safety, sales, accounts and conducting welcome meetings for guests arriving in the resort. The latter was the subject of a major assessment. Another major assessment followed an exercise conducted in the hotel where the course was being held. 'We had to carry out a health and safety assessment of the hotel, just as we would in overseas resorts and then discuss it with the hotel's general manager. They obviously wanted to know how good we would be at communicating with managers. One girl was failed for being too aggressive and had to leave.' Gemma was told on the last afternoon that she had passed the course successfully and would be going to Gran Canaria. She was happy about this as she had studied Spanish while at university, and had therefore asked to go to a Spanish resort.

Gemma spent two-and-a-half years at the Gran Canaria Princess Hotel where she was very happy. 'All the staff were fantastic and really helpful.' There is a lot of sales work in a resort rep's job. They have to encourage guests to book for excursions and evening entertainment. Gemma says that she spent about half of her time looking after guests and the other half in selling – with high targets to achieve. 'In the hotel I would sell excursions, advise on car hire and recommend places to see, deal with any problems regarding the hotel, and do everything possible to help the guests have a good holiday. Outside the hotel I had meet-and-greet duties when I would accompany a group of departing guests to the airport and help them to check in, then I would go to arrivals to meet a new group, check that all were there and had their luggage, then take them to the hotel, giving them some information about the resort on the way. I would help at reception at check in and see that everyone had the correct room allocated. Every week I went through both flight and room lists to make sure that if there were any people who had booked late they were not without a room. In addition, I was the guide on some excursions and nights out. There was a lot of paperwork and it all had to be done accurately, otherwise I would have had problems! I also had to keep accounts for all the excursions.

We were monitored constantly on our performance on both the sales and customer service side. Information was available from our sales figures and also from satisfaction questionnaires that guests completed. I actually felt that my two roles went hand in hand. Even if I was selling, I was still trying to make sure that people enjoyed themselves.'

After 18 months Gemma was promoted to guest services manager, which meant dealing with particular issues or handling problems other reps passed to her. 'I would visit any guests who were in hospital, for instance, arrange compensation if anyone had requested a sea view and had not been given one, might translate where it was necessary, even evict guests who were causing problems! I enjoyed this role and felt I was really using my people skills.'

## Worldwide travel

However, Gemma decided to move on and applied for an air cabin crew position with Virgin Atlantic. Thomson were very good and let her arrange her winter break to coincide with the interviews. Virgin's selection process consisted of several group-work exercises, designed to see how well applicants worked in a team and were willing to help each other. There were also English and arithmetic tests, and an individual interview during which Gemma's background and skills in customer service were thoroughly explored. She was informed the next day that she had been accepted and negotiated a starting date that would allow her to complete her winter season with Thomson. 'I didn't want to let them down, and besides, I had been in the position of having a new rep arrive once mid-season, which meant that she needed a lot of support. I didn't think it fair to my colleagues in the resort to do this.'

Training for her new job took six weeks – on a very intensive course with a test every day on what had been covered so far. 'I had never done anything like this before! No previous course or exam had been such hard work.'

Airlines have their own training programmes – which vary slightly but all trainees obviously have to learn about safety, procedures, equipment and aviation medicine. Since there is a detailed description of the training BA steward Eddy Tumath followed on page 225, Gemma's training is not covered in depth here.

Gemma stayed with Virgin Atlantic for ten months, during which time she flew to places all over the world, including South America, South Africa, the Caribbean, the west coast of the USA, Florida, Hong Kong, Sydney and Nigeria – with stopovers at each one.

## Out of tourism for a while

She then decided that she wanted a more settled lifestyle and her next move took her to London, where she worked as a recruitment consultant – another customer-service role. It wasn't the sort of job she wanted, however; she wanted to get back into leisure or tourism.

## Return to tourism

So her next job was with Tourism South East (one of the regional tourist boards) in Eastleigh, Hampshire, near Southampton. 'This is my favourite of the jobs I've done in the UK. I was a key-account executive covering Surrey and Sussex. My job was to liaise with all the major hotels and tourist attractions that were members, and contact others and persuade them to join. I then kept them informed of changes and updates that they needed to know about – one example was the no-smoking legislation. I ensured that they knew about health and safety, and fire regulations, and so on, but my main role was to look after all their marketing and publicity needs, and in doing so, to increase the popularity of the South East as a tourist destination. I could offer them different grades of marketing package, depending on their needs and the price they wished to pay. Packages ranged from £250 a year to £5,000. I loved that job. I was in constant contact with the clients and I had to keep in touch with all the media – newspapers, television and radio, and do some advertising work too.'

## Another move

'I was sorry to leave, but my roots are in the North East and I decided recently that I wanted to move back there. So I have moved from tourism to leisure again. I will go back and complete my tourism degree one day – but not just yet.'

## Career note

Resort representatives are recruited and trained by individual holiday operators, that each have their own entry requirements. There are no standard ones, although most companies expect GCSE maths. There are no standard entry requirements for jobs with tourism authorities. A formal qualification in tourism is not always required if applicants have relevant experience, as Gemma had.

You can find out how to become an air cabin crew member by reading the career profile of Eddy Tumath on page 225.

## Further information

**TTC Training** – The Quayside, 4 Furnival Road, Sheffield S4 7YA. Tel: 0800 915 9396. www.ttctraining.co.uk

**The Institute of Travel and Tourism** – PO Box 217, Ware, Herts SG12 8WY. Tel: 0870 770 7960. www.itt.co.uk

## Related careers

Courier

Tour guide

Tourist Information Centre work

# Henry Marshall
## Air traffic control assistant – National Air Traffic Services (NATS)

Henry is employed by National Air Traffic Services (NATS), a public/private partnership that employs the majority of controllers working at British airports. Air traffic controllers are responsible for the movement of aeroplanes along the major air routes and on the ground at airports. They monitor aircraft movements, calculate safe distances and give instructions to pilots. Controllers work in watches, or shifts, helped by air traffic control assistants.

### Henry's job

Henry works at the air traffic control centre at Swanwick in Hampshire, in a team that controls the North Sea sector. 'I don't have any direct control over aircraft, but I am responsible for passing on very important information accurately. Air traffic controllers have flight progress strips in front of them all the time that an aircraft is in their area. The strips are generated by computer and hold all the information that is needed for every aircraft that is on their screen – type, altitude, departure point, destination, call sign, times of reaching reporting points (entry, mid point and end of sector). The strips are prepared in advance as flight plans have to be filed four hours before take off, but the information may have to be changed if the controller has to re-route an aircraft for any reason. A controller can sometimes have more than ten aircraft on the screen at any one time. My job is to get the strips to the controller, and remove them as soon as the aircraft has been handed on to the next controller.

The printers are all next to the assistants' positions. To anyone watching it might look as though all I do is take bits of paper out of the printer, but I have to make decisions on which order to give them to the controller if two or three arrive straight after one another – and I have to answer the phone. There is a lot of military activity over the North Sea in addition to heavy transatlantic traffic, and we get frequent requests for military pilots to enter our air space or to be given priority over a civil aircraft due to enter. I have to give the message to the controller then pass the answer back. I can't afford a mistake! At busy times, I have to prioritise and make instant decisions about which to deal with first, the strips or the phone.'

## Working hours

Henry works shifts round the clock on a ten-day cycle. It is planned in advance, but could change if he was needed to cover for someone else's absence. It means constant adjustments for the body clock, and he does get tired at times. He has now worked out some ways to cope – like sleeping for as long as possible in the day before a night shift. He is also allowed some choice of shift where possible.

## First career steps

Henry has been interested in aviation for a long time. 'I always had pictures of aircraft in my room.' At school he was an air cadet and he organised his school work experience with the Civil Aviation Authority (CAA). This enabled him to spend some time at the air traffic control centre in West Drayton.

He took A levels at his school, Howard of Effingham, and achieved passes in A level physics and AS electronics. Computer studies and pure maths did not go so well, so Henry, who had put in a UCAS application for computer studies, abandoned that idea and moved to Guildford College to re-take some A levels. By now, however, he had become keen on psychology, and therefore took that at A level plus AS statistics. He duly applied for psychology, but when the A level results came out, although he had respectable grades in both subjects, they were not high enough for his first choice of university.

Henry now reconsidered his career plans and decided that he was more motivated towards work. He went to work for a wine merchant and 18 months later was the assistant manager of the branch. 'In actual fact I was the manager – because he left and was not replaced!' The job was not very inspiring, however, and when Henry's mother, who works for the CAA, saw in her staff magazine that NATS were advertising for trainee air traffic control assistants he decided to apply.

## Selection

The first stage was a fairly standard application form containing the usual questions on qualifications, interests and reasons for choosing the career. Henry is convinced that the care he took over the last section is the factor that made the selectors shortlist him for interview. 'I wrote a lot about my interest in aviation and described my visit to West Drayton and what I had learned there. I found out later that NATS always receive a large number of applications when they advertise. Well over 60 applicants were invited for interview.'

The interview was a mix of questions and spot tests. Henry was asked detailed questions about aviation – What types of aircraft fly across the Atlantic? What do the numbers marked on runways mean? – and was given pen-and-paper maths questions to do there and then. 'For instance, I was given one question to work out regarding which of two aircraft was nearer to the terminal, given their distances and travelling speeds. Another consisted of a list of four digit numbers. I had to circle the ones that appeared more than once. I had to do all the questions with the two interviewers watching me – so had to be conscious of the time factor while also aiming for accuracy.' One test he could not have done unless he had visited an air traffic control centre. 'I was given a flight progress strip and asked questions about it, for example, what type of plane it was and at what altitude it was flying.' He was also asked about his reasons for wishing to become a controller and for any evidence that he could work in a team.

## Training

Henry was accepted and joined a group of new trainees for a 12-week training course. All the new entrants had some form of aviation experience. Some were former air cabin-crew staff and RAF air traffic controllers; one had a private pilot's licence; one was straight from university and had been an air cadet. Henry and one other had A levels.

The first three weeks were spent in a classroom. 'We worked through a big manual of air traffic services, covering sector information, altitudes of different airways, aircraft types and performance. There was a lot to learn. There was an exam at the end of each week and we had to get

70% to pass.' In addition to the theory, the group also did some team-building exercises.

The remainder of Henry's three-month training period was spent learning on the job. He was assigned to the North Sea sector and at first watched an experienced assistant at work before very quickly doing small parts of the work. 'There was always a trainer behind me – but towards the end of my training he was just watching me do the job myself.'

In order to become *validated* or qualified, Henry had another exam to pass – this time a 45-minute oral followed by a 45-minute assessment of his work. He then moved onto training on a second sector. 'This training took less time because I already knew the job. This was just covering sector-specific knowledge.'

## The next step

Where does Henry go from here? National Air Traffic Services assistants can apply to become air traffic controllers whenever they feel that they are ready to do the job. They take a series of tests designed to assess spatial awareness, decision-making ability, mental arithmetic and personality, plus several interviews. There is also a written exam on a manual that applicants are sent and expected to know thoroughly before applying for an exam date. Henry has applied once but was unsuccessful. He will wait for a year and then apply again. 'Most people pass the second time', he says.

---

## Career note

To become an air traffic controller it is necessary to have excellent powers of concentration, a strong sense of responsibility and a calm, even temperament. Alertness and quick reactions are essential for coping with emergencies. Controllers should have a technical aptitude and the ability to learn to use radar and computer systems. A clear speaking voice is important and a liking for teamwork essential. Controllers usually work in the same teams, building up a strong rapport.

Entry requirements are a matter for individual employers. Most controllers work for NATS, but there are some airports owned by local authorities and some privately-owned airfields that employ their own controllers. To join NATS you would need five GCSEs/S grades at A*-C/1-3 including English and maths, and to have studied for A levels/Highers or an appropriate diploma. There are no standard requirements set by other airport owners. Some recruit only experienced personnel. Others state a requirement of five GCSEs/S grades at A\*-C/1-3 including maths, English and a science.

All entrants need a high standard of physical fitness and eyesight. Colour vision must be normal, and hearing and speech without defect. Controllers have to pass an annual medical in order to retain their licences.

## Further information

**National Air Traffic Services Ltd** – 4000 Parkway, Whiteley, Fareham, Hants PO15 7FL. Tel: 01489 616001. www.nats.co.uk

## Related careers

Coastguard

Merchant Navy deck or engineering officer

Pilot (civil aviation or HM Forces)

---

# Jo Cox
## Deck officer cadet – Merchant Navy

---

Jo left school in the West Midlands at the age of 16 and completed an engineering Apprenticeship with Land Rover. Although she gained an Advanced GNVQ (now applied A level) in engineering through day release as part of her training, she chose to join the Merchant Navy as a deck officer and is now doing a three-year training course with a shipping organisation. Why was this? 'All through school I always wanted to go to sea. I couldn't find out very much about shipping careers though. I found lots on the Royal Navy but nothing on the Merchant Navy. (The Merchant Navy covers all types of civilian shipping – both cargo and passenger vessels.) I didn't want to commit myself to several years in the Royal Navy at that age, so I chose engineering instead. But I was spending all my spare time and money on sailing and becoming more and more interested in navigation. Through that hobby I met lots of people with Merchant Navy backgrounds and decided to find out more. I found the British Shipping website (www.british-shipping.org), which had a list of all the companies that were recruiting, and wrote to 12 for information.'

Jo eventually made four job applications and received job offers from all four organisations. The Lloyd's Officer Cadet Scholarship scheme was her choice.

## Selection

Jo was interviewed by Chiltern Maritime, an organisation that recruits and administers cadet training on behalf of three companies – Trinity House, Lloyd's and the Conway Merchant Navy Trust. She remembers her interview as being very friendly, with about half the time being spent on questions and the remainder on giving her information about the training and about life at sea. She was asked her reasons for choosing a Merchant Navy career and for applying to the particular scheme. It was pointed out that she would be at sea for very long periods and was asked if she expected to feel homesick or would object to sharing a cabin with another cadet who would be a stranger. 'They asked a lot about my previous experience and wanted to know what was the longest period I had ever spent away from home. They explained a lot about life onboard ship – how the crews could be very small on some and would be multinational.'

Why did Jo choose the Lloyd's Officer Cadet Scholarship scheme? 'Because unlike most officer cadets I am sponsored rather than employed. I have a bursary from Lloyd's and my training is looked after by Chiltern Maritime. It means that I am not tied to any company. I get my sea experience with different ones, and when I finish training I shall be able to apply to any I choose. All the other cadets in my group are employed and therefore on a salary, but financially I am on a par with most of them and better off than some, because I don't pay tax or national insurance contributions.'

## College

Officer cadets follow a three-year sandwich course, which consists of periods at college followed by placements at sea. Jo began with a six-week induction course at the Warsash Maritime Centre, near Southampton, which trains cadets from several shipping companies. (There are four such colleges in the UK. She was allowed to choose the one she wished to attend, although some companies only use certain colleges.)

There is a good social life in the college – 'mainly because we are some distance from a town and so we do things on site or go out together in groups.' There is also the chance to meet cadets from other shipping companies. On this induction course, cadets learn basic shipboard workings and sea survival, which included a visit to a local swimming pool to practise righting life rafts, lifeboat handling and firefighting. There are excellent facilities. The college has its own lifeboats, and firefighting courses are held in the college's purpose built firefighting school.

## To sea

The second phase of Jo's training involved five-and-a-half months at sea. She spent this time with BP on a very large tanker. She should have stayed for four months, but was enjoying it so much that she asked to stay longer instead of doing a second, shorter trip. At sea, Jo first learned deck work. Some of it held little relevance to navigation, but Jo explains that it was necessary for her to learn everyone else's job in order to be able to instruct and lead others. So, she helped with repainting and minor maintenance on lifeboats and firefighting and cargo equipment. 'I loved the whole period. There were only 22 crew. I had my own cabin and everyone went out of their way to help with my training. It's in everyone's interests, of course, to make sure that all the crew members are competent in everything they do! After the first two weeks I started spending four hours of an eight-hour watch on the bridge with the mate, doing very simple tasks connected with navigation, and four more still working as a deckhand. As I became more competent I was given more responsible work to do, like assisting the officer of the watch during cargo operations in port. I would help to take measurements of tanks or open and close valves and keep the records up to date. It was all real work that somebody had to do – not something manufactured for a trainee to do.' During this period Jo also had to complete a portfolio of evidence for an NVQ.

## Back to college

Jo then had some leave before spending six months back at Warsash, studying the principles of navigation, electronic navigation aids, navigation and cargo work. By now, the work was becoming very demanding and Jo found her technical background useful. 'There was a lot of theory. We studied the construction of ships, stability, tides and celestial navigation, and also did further practical work – survival, safe use of lifeboats, more rope work, advanced firefighting and first aid.'

## On the bridge

Jo then did her second period of sea experience, this time with Bank Line, a general cargo company. 'That means that they transport all sorts of things – containers, lorries, oil, timber and miscellaneous items. I joined the ship in France. It was going to Tahiti and bakers there prefer French flour, so we had two holds full of bags of that.'

Jo's voyage took her round the world, through the Panama Canal and via New Zealand and the South Pacific, stopping at 'very small ports that few ships visit'. For the first month she worked in deck maintenance again. Then she started to do two four-hour watches a day, understudying the third officer on the bridge. The officer of the watch is responsible for all aspects of navigation, including monitoring radio communications, plotting the ship's position on the chart, looking out for other traffic, and altering the vessel's course whenever necessary according to weather or tide conditions. 'I plotted positions, monitored the weather, used radar and gradually learned to take responsibility for a watch, but under supervision'. Once again she had a single cabin.

Was she able to visit many ports? 'The captain was very good about letting the three cadets go ashore whenever possible, so I got at least half a day in most places'.

## More theory

Jo is now back at Warsash for three months, concentrating on radar, navigation, maritime law and management. Her next sea trip will be with the British Antarctic Survey – which she has specifically requested. When she is fully qualified she will apply to shipping companies for a position as a third officer.

Jo's training has been very thorough. It has to be. The safety of an entire ship will one day rest on her. Tests are held constantly at Warsash and, while she is at sea, she has to keep a log book recording the topics she has covered. This is signed by the captain. In addition to written examinations she will have an oral exam with Maritime and Coastguard Agency officials, covering navigation, collision rules and safety. She is studying for a Higher National Diploma in nautical science over three years. It is, however, the oral exam that will give her an Officer of the Watch Certificate – necessary for promotion to junior officer status.

The usual pattern of progression for deck officers is to gain periods of sea experience, then come ashore to study for the next certificate of competency, thus gaining promotion to second, first and chief officer. A number will finally attain the rank of captain.

## Career note

To join the officer cadet training scheme at Jo's level, candidates must have five GCSEs/S grades at A*-C/1-3, including English, maths, and physics or combined science, plus A levels or Highers in any subject (120 UCAS points are required). Applicants attend an interview and must pass a medical examination and an eye test.

There are also engineering officer and electro-technical officer cadet schemes for which science A levels/Highers or National/Advanced Diplomas in engineering subjects are acceptable. Training usually commences in September. You should apply to companies between September and March in the school year before you hope to start. Contact the Merchant Navy Training Board to find out which companies are recruiting or sponsoring.

Training has changed very recently. Cadets now follow a foundation degree programme, which in addition to the degree itself, gives them professional seafaring certificates of competency that permit them to work on board any ship, anywhere in the world. Training lasts approximately three years, and usually consists of three college phases and two sea phases, although this may vary according to the college and the sponsoring company.

## Further information

**Chamber of Shipping** – Merchant Navy Training Board, Carthusian Court, 12 Carthusian Street, London EC1M 6EZ. Tel: 0800 085 0973. www.mntb.org.uk

Contact individual shipping companies.

## Related careers

Airline pilot

Merchant Navy engineering officer

# Eddy Tumath
## Cabin crew member – British Airways

Eddy, who has Highers in maths, computing, accounts and finance, modern studies and English, had always wanted to do his present job. 'I've wanted it for as long as I can remember', he says.

Having such a clear goal Eddy planned his career path very carefully. He knew that he was unlikely to be accepted by British Airways (BA) before he was 21 and also knew that he would need experience of dealing with the public in a customer-service role. So he spent four years working in a travel agency, gaining both customer-service experience and knowledge of the travel industry. When he saw on the internet that BA were recruiting cabin crew he applied immediately, filling in an online application form. (BA and several other airlines only accept online applications.) Soon afterwards he received a phone call inviting him to an assessment day at BA's Heathrow training centre.

## Selection

Eddy spent a whole day doing tests and interviews. 'There were about 20 of us and we were divided into three smaller groups. Each group did some group exercises and then had individual interviews. The group tasks were to assess our potential for team work. One of the things we had to do was plan a promotional day for a company's valued clients. We had a list of about 30 possible activities and details of the clients, who included single and married people, some of whom had families, and some people who had disabilities. Bearing all these factors in mind, and sticking to a budget, we had to arrive at a group decision. After the group work I had a 45-minute interview with two interviewers who took it in turns to ask the questions. These were very detailed. I was asked in-depth questions about my career to date and had to give examples of situations in which I had done particularly good work and had gone over and above the call of duty in order to help customers. I was also asked about my reasons for applying to BA and what I thought made the company stand out from others. There were also some written tests in information handling and in arithmetic. Three days later I heard that I had been accepted.'

## Training

Eddy's initial training consisted of six weeks spent in the training school. During this time he lived in bed and breakfast accommodation near Heathrow. Training was intensive. There was a lot to absorb on the technical features of the aircraft and on safety and evacuation procedures. The training centre was equipped with cabins and galleys for practice in cabin service and simulated emergency situations. Trainees took turns in acting the part of passengers while the others learned to deal with potential problems and difficult or unwell passengers. Safety equipment and procedures were covered fully. 'We had state-of-the-art cabin mockups', says Eddy, 'where we learned everything from how to fight fires to dealing with a bomb threat or evacuating an aircraft. During one session we had to deal with a simulated emergency situation. Some people sat in passenger seats, then the cabin was suddenly filled with smoke and we had to deal with putting out a fire, preparing for an emergency landing and evacuating all the 'passengers'.'

Evacuation procedures over water were learned in a swimming pool where the trainees had to inflate a life raft while wearing their life jackets, then help other people into the rafts. Eddy found aviation medicine particularly interesting. 'We covered first aid, learned how to carry out resuscitation – both manually and with defibrillators – and learned which types of medication were carried on board, which ones we could administer and which ones we could do under authorisation from BA's medical advisers. There is a medical company that we can ring at any time by satellite phone and they tell us what to do and whether we need to ask the question 'Is there a doctor on board?' My new skills were of use soon after I had done this part of the course when I went out with a group of friends and one fainted in the restaurant. I was the one who knew what to do!'

## First flight

At the end of the six-week training period Eddy had his first flight – not as a trainee or supernumerary staff member, but as a full member of the team. How did he feel? 'Very nervous. I knew that I had been trained for every possible eventuality but there is always the feeling that however much training you have had, it isn't enough. As it happened, the work came naturally and everything I had learned fell into place. My colleagues were really helpful and all were willing to take time to help me if I needed it.'

Eddy was not yet fully qualified, however. He had to work for six months and 'earn his wings'. After receiving good assessments and attending a refresher course at Gatwick he was allowed to wear silver wings on his uniform jacket and lost his probationer status. Once each year he will return to the training centre to undertake a refresher course.

## Duties

Eddy now flies out of Gatwick, travelling down on BA domestic flights from his home in Aberdeen before he starts a duty period. He receives his roster well in advance and knows when his working days and days off will be in a six-week period. He flies mainly to the USA and Caribbean countries and has stopovers there of between one and four days between flights. 'I normally get three days off at the end of every trip. This is because my flights are usually about eight hours in length. If I worked at Heathrow where flights are more varied I would get from two days after a short flight to five after going to Australia. How I spend my time on stopovers depends on where I am. In the USA I do a lot of shopping. In Antigua, Bermuda or Barbados I spend more time on the beach or by the hotel pool. There are usually two BA crews in a hotel at the same time, so we have plenty of company. In fact we almost become like each others' families because we are together constantly over a period of several days.'

Cabin crew are rostered for duty by computer, which means that they do not know who they will be working with or whether they will be with colleagues they have worked with previously. Eddy usually finds that, because smaller numbers are based at Gatwick than at Heathrow, he usually knows one or two of the team already.

Before each flight, cabin crew meet in the briefing room where they are given information on the flight and told by the cabin services director how many passengers will be on the flight and whether any have particular requirements such as special diets or wheelchairs. Duties are allocated, but staff are allowed to choose, in order of seniority, whether they want to work in first, club world or world traveller class. the cabin services director then holds snap tests! He asks questions on safety and medical procedures to test the staff's knowledge and make sure that everyone is competent.

The crew are then bussed or walk to the aircraft and prepare the cabins for boarding. 'We do a safety and equipment check and inspect passenger seatback pockets, overhead lockers and the floor to make certain that no one has left behind anything that could be suspicious. We also prepare as much as we can in the galleys, and load trolleys with snacks and drinks to speed up meal and bar service later. Then we board the passengers – welcome them, check their boarding cards to make sure that they are on the right aircraft, ensure that luggage is properly stowed before take off and do the safety demonstrations and explanations.' The work is physically demanding. In the air the cabin crew are on their feet constantly, serving meals and drinks, selling duty-free goods and generally attending to passengers' needs. On a long flight, there should be the opportunity to get some rest in rows of seats reserved for crew use at the rear of the aircraft. When the passengers have disembarked they do more safety checks, once again making sure that equipment is in the right place and that no suspicious objects have been left behind.

Has the job lived up to Eddy's expectations? 'Yes in every way! It's a fantastic job and British Airways is a fantastic company to work for.

Every flight is different. The passengers are different and nothing is routine. Even when you are doing the standard trolley service, things crop up. One passenger might point out to you that a seat-back video screen isn't working, or someone might need medication. I get to meet so many fascinating people from all over the world – both passengers and colleagues. And I get to visit interesting places and stay in excellent hotels.'

## The future

Eddy intends to stay with BA for his entire career – and in due course would like to become a cabin services director.

## Advice from Eddy

'Don't worry if you are not accepted by a major airline for your first job. I was lucky and didn't make any other applications. Some people feel that they would not want to work for a small company with few routes. But by doing so, they would gain valuable experience and could apply to other companies later on.'

## Career note

Entry requirements vary with different airlines. Most expect applicants to have previous experience of dealing with the public, plus at least four GCSEs/S grades at A*-C/1-3. Knowledge of foreign languages is useful – although not always necessary, since many airlines employ cabin staff of all nationalities, who between them speak many different languages.

## Further information

You can find the addresses of airlines in *Flight International Directory*, which should be in reference libraries, and on the internet.

## Related careers

Resort representative

Tour manager (courier)

Tour guide

Tourist Information Centre work

# Alex Hargreaves
## Advanced Apprentice (commercial) – Bentley Motors

Alex, who has A levels in economics, environmental science and graphics, plus AS level IT, is in the third year of an Advanced Apprenticeship with Bentley Motors in Crewe.

He always knew that he did not want full-time higher education, but did not know what kind of career he wanted to follow. So during his A level course at Sir John Deane's Sixth Form College in Northwich, Cheshire, he consulted with the careers team regularly to discuss alternative career paths. Although the majority of students from the college do move on to full-time degree courses, there was, he says, no pressure put on him to follow that route. 'They respect your own decision and are there to help you with information and help.' Alex had a lot of contact with the team who provided him with information about the options open to him and the types of employer he could approach. He found the head of careers, who also taught him economics, particularly helpful. 'I don't think that I was his most studious pupil, but I was probably one of the most entertaining and we got on well. We had a lot of conversations, which helped me to work out that I wanted some kind of business career and although he didn't push me towards a particular employer, he was keen that I should work for a large company where I would receive good training and plenty of career opportunities.'

The actual choice of company, however, was a lucky coincidence. Alex was actually on the internet reading about careers when he saw that Bentley Motors had an Apprenticeship scheme – and an online application form.

## Application and selection

This process took some time. Alex first downloaded the form and completed it. He then discussed it with careers staff before completing the final version. Several weeks later he was requested to send his CV. Again, he asked for suggestions from staff when compiling it. Eventually he was invited to attend a selection day.

First came maths and English tests. These were followed by a competency-based interview. 'The first questions were general ones and were about me as a person. I was asked things like how I liked to spend my free time, for example. Then they became specific and were related to the competencies related to the job I would be doing. I had to answer questions like Can you work in a team? Have you ever restructured a team? Have you ever had to achieve targets – and, if so, how? Have you any experience of managing other people? I had to think, but soon realised that I could come up with examples. My part-time job supplied most of them. While at college I worked in a restaurant. I ran the service side really, while my boss concentrated on the finance and budgeting. I had six or seven people reporting to me. So I used examples of dealing with both staff and customers – and resolving some of the issues that arose. You get plenty of them in customer service.' These experiences and Alex's good understanding of the automotive industry all helped. Alex was accepted and started work.

## Early days

On his first day, together with other new employees who had also joined that day, Alex followed an induction programme consisting of presentations from different speakers. 'They all came from different departments, so the presentations covered general topics about the company and about terms of employment. We heard about the company's work and current goals (which are re-set every 12 months), about holiday entitlement, company cars and the pension scheme, and had a tour of the factory. The next day I was given a more detailed introduction to the work of my department.'

## Logistics

'My Apprenticeship has the title 'commercial apprentice', but covers the wider area of logistics. My first placement within Bentley was within the logistics supply-chain planning team, where I was responsible for implementing and maintaining effective supply-chain management for a third of the Continental Flying Spur suppliers.

After 12 months I requested experience in sales and marketing as I wanted to gain greater commercial awareness. It was a very good placement. I learned a lot – particularly about work with external customers, as opposed to the internal customers I had been dealing with until then. Within the role I worked in the after-sales department project managing the delivery of a new range of accessories to support the launch of the continental GTC.

I am now back in pre-series logistics, where I am doing project management. It is our responsibility to support the project in its on-time delivery. It touches all areas of the business and we work closely with engineering, quality control and purchasing departments. We have to ensure that all the suppliers are up to speed and will have the correct tooling and get their timing right. We also manage the engineering change and development to ensure that we fit the latest level parts.'

## Training

All Alex's training to date has been on the job. When he joined the company he was assigned a mentor – an experienced member of staff who is his guide, who advises him on his training and can help to organise or plan different aspects of it. 'For example, I asked him about the sales placement and he was instrumental in setting it up.' Do they meet regularly? 'Yes, but not through regular, pre-arranged meetings. Some mentors and trainees meet at fixed times but I have a more informal relationship with my mentor. We talk as often as we need to. We also have to work jointly on my progress reports, which go to the personnel office.'

Training at Bentley Motors is flexible. Under the terms of his Apprenticeship agreement Alex has to work towards an NVQ level 3 in procurement. For this he has to provide a portfolio of evidence as he successfully completes a task from a list of given topics – which include, for example, 'Negotiating improvements in supplier performance', and 'Maintaining the effectiveness of procurement operations'. Once or twice he has felt that he needed to return to departments he'd worked in previously in order to acquire some more experience – and he has easily been able to do so.

Alex says that he has a great deal of freedom to organise much of his own training. 'There are guidelines that I should follow and I have to do the NVQ work obviously. But I am under no pressure at present to take any external courses. There is a whole range of things I could do, and people have already started to mention HNCs – but I do not feel ready yet to undertake one and I have not decided what it will be. When the time comes I will be able to do an HNC or degree programme with full support from the company – and I could choose from business studies, financial planning, purchasing and supply, or even do a full degree in logistics.'

## Finance

How does Alex manage financially? 'I have an associate car, and I can choose to contribute 4-6% of my salary to the company pension scheme, which is matched by Bentley. I haven't much to complain about! And I am not building up any student debt.'

## Alex's advice

'If, like me, you don't want to do a full-time degree course but don't know exactly what you do want, you really must get some careers advice – and then act on it. Look up all the things the staff suggest – and use their help also when it comes to CVs and application forms.' Alex has just been asked to give a talk at his former college's careers day to be held later in the year.

## Career note

Other companies offer similar schemes, but availability will depend very much on where you live. There are usually opportunities in large companies to work for professional qualifications in, for example, purchasing, marketing or general business administration, or to take a relevant degree course. Apprenticeships provide the opportunity to obtain an NVQ level 3 or 4 qualification.

## Further information

For information on Apprenticeships and companies offering training in your local area, contact your Connexions/careers service.

# Chapter sixteen

# Working for yourself

## Roger Chunnoo
### Partner – Country Heritage Insurance Agencies

Roger and his partner, Sheree McCrory, own a business that employs four other staff, and in its second year of trading will achieve a £750,000 turnover.

Eighteen months ago, both were working for a small insurance firm but becoming increasingly disillusioned about future career prospects, they spotted a gap in the market and decided to go it alone. Roger at that time was a junior member of staff. Sheree was the office manager.

### Background

Roger attended St Helena's Comprehensive school in Colchester where he gained A levels in law and politics. He had also started A level maths with the idea of becoming a pilot, but disliked the subject and abandoned the idea of becoming a pilot.

When he left school he had no firm career plans and took a 'temporary' job in a pub. The job lasted two years until one day one of the regular customers asked him if he was going to work behind a bar for ever and offered him a job in his insurance firm. 'It seemed like a good idea, but at 21 I had to take a cut in salary and do what was basically office-junior work, including mountains of filing.'

Roger stayed with the firm for four years. By then he had been trained in general insurance work and had passed the first two stages of the Chartered Insurance Institute's examinations.

## The company

Heritage Insurance arranges insurance cover for buildings with timber frames and/or thatched roofs. Owners of such properties normally find insurance cover hard to obtain and expensive, as few companies deal in this area. 'Many firms just aren't interested in offering anything other than easy to arrange, straightforward cover.' Roger and Sheree decided that by becoming specialists they would be able to negotiate terms with insurance providers and offer competitive terms to clients. Basically, they act as the intermediaries between a client wanting cover and an insurance company that is willing to provide it. 'We design a policy based on the standard household or contents-cover policy used by most insurers, but altered to take account of the special risks these properties have.

Normally clients contact us by phone. We ask some basic questions such as date of birth (older clients usually get cheaper insurance) and postcode – the insurance industry has some standard statistics that assess the risk of theft or subsidence by area. We also have to assess any unusual risks and ask about the history of the building, for example, Have there been any fires or floods? How much thatch is there? Has the property been extended? Interestingly, old buildings that are built without foundations don't usually suffer from subsidence. It is when you add a modern extension that problems can occur and part of the building moves.

We can offer a quote over the phone and if the client agrees to this, we send the forms for completion. When they are returned we have to check them carefully, then forward them to the insurers together with the client's cheque. We then receive a percentage of the policy cost in commission.'

## Starting out

The two were confident of their ability in insurance, but they had no experience of running a business. So before leaving their permanent employment they attended evening courses in book-keeping and business planning. Then they had to find backers.

'We had to find an insurance company to take us on. We went to business meetings with several, to market ourselves. We had a lot of nerve! There I was in my early twenties in meetings with people thirty years older and all I could offer was promises – 'If you accept us, I can assure you we will be good' – that kind of thing. Eventually we ended up with Lloyd's of London.' (This isn't actually a company but a number of different firms, known as syndicates, working at Lloyd's premises.)

The evening class lecturer had some leaflets from LiveWIRE (see page 82). They saw a competition for the business plan of the year and sent theirs in. That year they were finalists in the pre-trading section. (The following year they won the New Trading Award.) The prize was £500, which they put towards their start-up costs. They obtained a £3,000 loan from The Prince's Trust (see page 82) and the remaining money they needed came from their own savings and family loans. This year they are using the £1,000 they won from LiveWIRE to buy a new computer.

At first, they did everything themselves, 'including a pet hate, filing' and all the book-keeping, often working into the early hours. Now they employ their own book-keeper and an outside accountant to prepare their end-of-year accounts.

## Premises

At present they work in a converted garage with an added extension at Sheree's home. There isn't enough desk space and so they cannot all be there at the same time. However, two of their staff are part time, and Roger is out a great deal, generating business and often works from home.

This year they are planning to rent small premises. 'It will be much more efficient. We are spending a fortune in fax, email and phone bills just to keep in touch with each other.'

## Generating business

This is mainly Roger's province while Sheree manages the office side. He advertises all over the UK, in the press and *Yellow Pages*, designs mailshots and spends time visiting brokers who could introduce potential clients.

Sheree, though, is very good at spotting – and winning – competitions, which bring good press coverage. They have won a Royal Mail award for their mailshots and several new-business awards. They have also been finalists in the insurance industry's own awards for the best new product, competing against some major companies. All this has brought them publicity in the local press, radio and on cable TV.

## Expansion

They are just about to move into commercial policy work. Roger has plans to move into the insurance of thatched pubs and restaurants. 'This will mean designing a new policy because they have all kinds of risks associated with their line of business – loss of stock, theft, employee and client liability, security and so on.' Sheree is developing a messaging and secretarial service for small businesses, which can be run by herself and their present employees.

## Advice from Roger

'You must be really dedicated to run your own business. We often had to work until 4am when we started. Most important of all, before you even consider going it alone, you must be very confident of your product. We did know about insurance.

I have had no regrets, although we have had some sleepless nights! I couldn't go back now to working for someone else. I enjoy being my own boss and I like the flexibility to take a long lunch break or an afternoon off and catch up with work later.'

## Career note

It is possible to enter the insurance industry with level 3 qualifications and to study for professional qualifications.

## Further information

**The Chartered Insurance Institute** – www.insurancecareers.cii.co.uk

For information on self employment, see Chapter six.

# Stuart Ebdy
## Company owner

Stuart did extremely well in his Highers at Breadalbane Academy, Aberfeldy. He took English, chemistry, history, maths and physics over two years, plus a crash course in accounts and economics in year 2. The pressure was on for him to go to university. Stuart didn't want to do this. 'I had toyed with several career ideas in the past – from being a doctor to a police officer to an architect. I still didn't know what I wanted to do, but throughout my school life the idea of running my own business kept cropping up. Even at primary school I had wanted to achieve and my reports used to say that I was competitive and wanted to be the best. (This wasn't seen as a good thing!) At 17 the idea of running my own business took over firmly. In fact, in the action plan section of my Record of Achievement I stated 'After university I want to work in a large company, gain experience and develop my business skills. When I have sufficient knowledge I intend to set up my own business.' The only problem was that I did not know what sort of business to aim for.'

## A false start

As a compromise Stuart decided to do a degree course in entrepreneurship. 'That would keep everybody happy.' He duly applied to Aberdeen University, was accepted and started the course. Things began to go wrong. 'I hadn't worked very hard at school. I had achieved A grades because I had a good memory and could learn things just before exams. At university, lectures were not compulsory so I didn't go to many! I concentrated on having a good time instead. This meant that I had no knowledge to call on in the exam room and I failed the first year. I repeated it and failed again. As a result I had to leave. Although at the time things weren't looking too good, I don't regret failing university, as the whole experience forced me to grow up and realise that things weren't given to me on a plate.'

## First job

Stuart previously had a part-time job handing out flyers and leaflets for pubs and clubs, and had also done some promotional work in local supermarkets. He now decided to approach the company that produced this publicity material and enquire about the possibility of a full-time job. He was offered one and went to work there. His aim was to work his way up through the company, which he succeeded in doing. At the age of 19 he was in charge of the 22 staff who distributed the publicity material. His next move was into administration. 'At 20 I had gained a lot of experience and felt I knew a lot about running the company. I had given up all ideas of self-employment now and intended to make a career there. I had all sorts of ideas, which I kept putting to my bosses. BUT – they weren't going to listen to a 20 year old when they had been running things successfully for some time! I was happy in my job as an account handler, however, and would have stayed if another opportunity hadn't arisen after I had been there two years.

I am also a qualified sailing instructor and was offered a job for the summer, teaching sailing in islands off the West Coast. It was a hard decision, because it meant giving up my job, and would also mean contacting my manager at the publicity company later on to see if they could take me back again. I took the job though – I knew that I would always regret it if I didn't and I had a wonderful time travelling around the islands. It was a good summer – fun and well paid.

In mid-August my former manager rang and told me that they were going into liquidation and wouldn't be able to take me back. So what now? I returned to Aberdeen where I immediately received a few job offers. Then in a flash it came to me that now was the time to set up that business I had always thought about.'

## Enterprise

Stuart did not waste any time. He did some research on the internet one Sunday, attended an introductory business course organised by Business Gateway the following day, and on the Tuesday registered his first limited company!

'I realised that with the winding up of the company I had previously worked for there had to be a gap in the market and that I would have to act quickly. Freshers' week was about to start at the university and there would be a need for clubs and pubs to advertise. I used all my previous contacts – clients and printers – and went ahead.' Business Gateway staff had told Stuart about the Prince's Scottish Youth Business Trust (PSYBT) and he successfully obtained a loan of £2,500. In order to do so he had to go for an interview at which he had to present a business plan and prove that he had no funding from any other source. He was also put in touch with Shell LiveWIRE and was matched with one of their business advisers.

Even today, Stuart – who has just turned 25 and has five companies – has no other loans or overdrafts. He has a horror of debt, having seen too much being accrued by students and does not want to get into a situation where he owes money. 'I made a bit of a mess of my own finances as a student, and decided that, as that certainly had not been a good experience, I would not want to run a business in a similar way.'

Stuart's first company was White Sparks, an online printing business, which supplies business cards, flyers, posters, leaflets, brochures, booklets, tickets, greetings cards and many other printed products. Stuart acts as an intermediary. He receives orders from clients and passes them to printers. It is a good idea and one that works. 'I get in the orders and pass all of them on. It means that my customers get a good deal, the printers get orders without having to market themselves – and I take a profit.'

He owns the majority of White Sparks and is the managing director of four other companies that he has set up and in which he has sold some shares. 'I have interests in East Coast Interactive (a web development and software company), On-line Print and Design, Silver Leaf Clothing (which organises things like promotional T-shirts for sponsored events), an investment company and a new one in the pipeline, which is still under wraps.'

The investment company Windward Capital Ltd, is concerned with helping young people to develop their own companies. 'I received the backing I needed from Business Gateway who gave me all the information and advice I needed on tax and the legal implications of running a business. If they knew the answer they gave it straight away and if not they would find out and come back to me. I also had a business adviser through LiveWIRE who I could consult at any time. As a result I could develop my business without any worries on those aspects. I have decided that I could do a lot to help people on the practical side of starting up a business. They sell a share of their business to Windward, and in return they can benefit in learning from my experience and getting some hands-on help.'

Stuart has six employees, four full time and two part time, whom he moves around his different companies as needed. Windward Capital he runs by himself. He has been nominated for, and has won, several business and entrepreneurship awards. As a way of giving something back in return for the publicity and assistance he has received, he gives up some of his time to give talks for these organisations. 'They provided me with real assistance – and all the publicity I received brought me more networking opportunities. Therefore I like to do my bit to convince young people that it is perfectly possible to establish their own businesses with very little capital.'

## Advice from Stuart

'There is a lot of free advice available. Make use of it to learn all about the practical side of running a business.'

## Further information

For information on self employment, see Chapter six.

# More titles in the Student Helpbook series ...

*New Edition*
## CVs and Applications

For anyone who is applying for a job or college place; includes details of the Internet and how to use it in marketing yourself.

£11.99          ISBN: 978 1904979203

*New Edition*
## Excel at Interviews

This highly successful book makes invaluable reading for students and jobhunters.

£11.99          ISBN: 978 1904979227

## Careers with an Arts or Humanities Degree
Published in association with UCAS

Compulsory reading for anyone considering arts or humanities at degree level.

£11.99          ISBN: 978 1904979067

## Careers with a Science Degree
Published in association with UCAS

Concise and up-to-date look at the wide range of careers open to science graduates.

'*...one of the best careers books I have ever read*' Newscheck

£11.99          ISBN: 978 1904979074

## A Year Off ... A Year On?
Published in association with UCAS

All the information and advice you need on how to make the most of your time out between courses or jobs.

£11.99          ISBN: 978 1902876863

## Student Life: A Survival Guide
Published in association with UCAS

Essential advice for students beginning or soon to begin university or college.
'*... will help you budget and get the most out of your time*' The Daily Mail

£11.99          ISBN: 978 1904979012

Visit our new, secure, e-shop website: **www.lifetime-publishing.co.uk** where you can  view our full range of resources, download sample pages, order and now buy resources online.